KILNS

DANIEL RHODES

Other books by the author:
Clay and Glazes for the Potter
Stoneware and Porcelain

CHILTON BOOK COMPANY

KILNS Design, Construction, and Operation

RADNOR, PENNSYLVANIA

All drawings and photographs by the author unless otherwise noted.

ISBN: 0-8019-5358-8

Library of Congress Catalog Card Number 68-57512
  Designed by Harry Eaby
Manufactured in the United States of America
  Second Printing, May 1969
  Third Printing, January 1971
  Fourth Printing, August 1971
  Fifth Printing, January 1973
  Sixth Printing, August 1974

For Saha

Author's Preface

Of all man's arts, ceramics deals most directly with earth, water, air and fire—those elements which the ancients considered the essentials of our world. The fire is the key. By its action the soft and formless clay is given hardness and permanence, and a range of color related to the colors of the primordial igneous landscape. Without a knowledge of the action of fire, the potter's craft would not exist. Nor would those almost infinitely numerous shards with which we piece together most of the material and spiritual records of early human history.

Kindling and controlling fire so as to bring its inferno to bear on objects made of clay was at first an art practiced without benefit of any well understood principles. From the primitive bonfire or pit kiln to the modern kiln a long development occurred, which was marked at every stage with experimentation, trial and error, and, no doubt, much discouragement and failure. Even today, with the availability of meters, pyrometers, and other instruments of control, a certain mystery attends kiln firings. And in spite of the efforts of specialists, a degree of uncertainty persists. This uncertainty may account for the fact that potters do not regard their kilns as other craftsmen might regard their tools; rather they look upon the kiln as a place of holocaust, a potential enemy and destroyer as well as collaborator. By and large the action of the kiln has given rise to considerable superstition, and firing has not been well understood, even by many who are otherwise well trained in ceramics.

There is a surprising lack of literature dealing with kilns, and this book is intended to bring together information which is widely scattered in various sources (or heretofore nonexistent) in a form which I hope will be useful to ceramists. It should be of special interest to those who contemplate building their own kilns.

But those who have no such bold idea may find information here to complete and extend their knowledge of the ceramic art.

This is written from the point of view of one who has built and fired kilns, rather than that of a theorist. My own lack of engineering knowledge precludes technical treatments of such subjects as combustion, heat transfer, and thermodynamics, but it is doubtful if the present work is the place for such discussion in any case. Those who desire more knowledge of the scientific aspects of kilns and firing will need to supplement this book with studies in other texts.

With some trepidation, I have included some dimensioned drawings for kilns as a guide to construction. While I believe these to be practical and workable designs, they carry no guarantee of success. So many variables are involved in the construction and operation of any kiln that experience, trial and error, and experimentation, rather than a fixed design, must be relied upon for success.

I wish to credit my wife Lillyan for her assistance in planning, organizing, and writing this book, and for her many insights that have enriched its contents.

I also wish to thank those who contributed photographs and data. I am indebted to David Cornell for his thoughtful reading of the manuscript and helpful suggestions.

Daniel Rhodes
Alfred, New York, 1968

Contents

AN ART OF FIRE

perfects
    the mystery,

completes
    the life-line of
    our common clay.

Potters transform
    like alchemists of old
  crude earth into *le pierre qui vive*
  F I R E I N T H E S T O N E.

They shape their kilns to tongues of flame,
    its food and rule,
pacing the flow of fuel, the hold of heat,
the cooling,
alert to tame the elemental blaze
                into life-vessel for
          Aquarian Man.

Self-creation is an art of fire:
         each person
         forms
         his spirit's housing
         and
         celestial cistern.

Mary Caroline Richards

PART 1

The Development of Kilns

1

Early Kilns

THE CERAMIC KILN was one of man's earliest tools, the primitive form of which dates back to at least 8000 B.C., and perhaps much earlier. The earliest kilns, however, were little more than modified bonfires. The exact style of kilns used in prehistoric times is conjectural, but it can be assumed that firing methods in the remote past were similar to those practiced by primitive peoples today.

The method of firing clay objects or vessels to make them hard, durable, and impervious to water was no doubt discovered accidentally. Perhaps men observed that the clay soils beneath the campfire became hardened by the heat. Or perhaps mudlined baskets were accidentally burned in fires, leaving the hardened liner in the form of a fired vessel. From such discoveries it would only be a small step to a more controlled management of the fire to gain concentrated heat applied to objects fashioned of clay. A knowledge of pottery making and of the technique of firing became widespread among primitive cultures, and was practiced in a very similar manner in areas as remote from each other as Central Asia and South America.

There are many local variations of open pit firing as practiced by primitive potters, but the essential procedure involves surrounding the pottery with red hot coals and embers, thus raising the temperature of the clay to red heat. To do this a shallow pit is dug into the ground, perhaps 14 to 20 inches deep and several square feet in area. Twigs, branches or reeds are placed in the pit, lining its sides and bottom. On this lining the pots are placed, piled together in a compact mass, with as little empty space between them as possible. Fuel is sometimes stacked in and around the pieces. Around and over the setting of raw pots is placed a layer

1. *Women potters of the Gwari Tribe, Northern Nigeria. A single pot is placed over a smoldering bed of coals preparatory to the firing. Photo by Peter Stichbury.*

of broken fragments of fired pottery, usually the broken pots from a previous firing, as shown in Figure 3. The fuel in the pit is set afire and allowed to burn rather slowly for an hour or two while the pottery becomes thoroughly dry. Since the fuel is in a shallow enclosure, not much air gets to it and at first the fire does not burn very intensely. Gradually, with the development of embers, heat begins to accumulate. More fuel is piled on, and as the fire builds up to a level above the pit it burns more fiercely. As more and more fuel is burned, a bed of red hot glowing embers surrounds the pottery, and the pottery itself begins to reach red heat. After the entire pit and its contents reach red heat, the fire is allowed to die down and the top of the fire may then be covered with wet leaves, dung or ashes to retain the heat. When the fire has died down and the embers have cooled, the finished pottery is taken from the pit. The broken pieces (usually a sizable percentage) are saved to use as the outer layer for the next firing.

1

Early Kilns

THE CERAMIC KILN was one of man's earliest tools, the primitive form of which dates back to at least 8000 B.C., and perhaps much earlier. The earliest kilns, however, were little more than modified bonfires. The exact style of kilns used in prehistoric times is conjectural, but it can be assumed that firing methods in the remote past were similar to those practiced by primitive peoples today.

The method of firing clay objects or vessels to make them hard, durable, and impervious to water was no doubt discovered accidentally. Perhaps men observed that the clay soils beneath the campfire became hardened by the heat. Or perhaps mudlined baskets were accidentally burned in fires, leaving the hardened liner in the form of a fired vessel. From such discoveries it would only be a small step to a more controlled management of the fire to gain concentrated heat applied to objects fashioned of clay. A knowledge of pottery making and of the technique of firing became widespread among primitive cultures, and was practiced in a very similar manner in areas as remote from each other as Central Asia and South America.

There are many local variations of open pit firing as practiced by primitive potters, but the essential procedure involves surrounding the pottery with red hot coals and embers, thus raising the temperature of the clay to red heat. To do this a shallow pit is dug into the ground, perhaps 14 to 20 inches deep and several square feet in area. Twigs, branches or reeds are placed in the pit, lining its sides and bottom. On this lining the pots are placed, piled together in a compact mass, with as little empty space between them as possible. Fuel is sometimes stacked in and around the pieces. Around and over the setting of raw pots is placed a layer

1. *Women potters of the Gwari Tribe, Northern Nigeria. A single pot is placed over a smoldering bed of coals preparatory to the firing. Photo by Peter Stichbury.*

of broken fragments of fired pottery, usually the broken pots from a previous firing, as shown in Figure 3. The fuel in the pit is set afire and allowed to burn rather slowly for an hour or two while the pottery becomes thoroughly dry. Since the fuel is in a shallow enclosure, not much air gets to it and at first the fire does not burn very intensely. Gradually, with the development of embers, heat begins to accumulate. More fuel is piled on, and as the fire builds up to a level above the pit it burns more fiercely. As more and more fuel is burned, a bed of red hot glowing embers surrounds the pottery, and the pottery itself begins to reach red heat. After the entire pit and its contents reach red heat, the fire is allowed to die down and the top of the fire may then be covered with wet leaves, dung or ashes to retain the heat. When the fire has died down and the embers have cooled, the finished pottery is taken from the pit. The broken pieces (usually a sizable percentage) are saved to use as the outer layer for the next firing.

2. *Women potters of the Gwari Tribe, Northern Nigeria. Pots are preheated over a very gentle fire and then placed over a bed of corn stalks and light twigs. In the final stage of firing, which takes about 1½ hours, dry grass is heaped over the fire to raise the temperature of the upper part of the setting. Photo by Peter Stichbury.*

3. *Open pit firing.*

4. *Preparing for a firing in an Indian Pueblo in New Mexico. The pottery, which has been polished, is placed on a rack over the fuel. Photo by Laura Gilpin.*

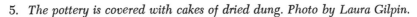

5. *The pottery is covered with cakes of dried dung. Photo by Laura Gilpin.*

6. *The fire begins to burn. Photo by Laura Gilpin.*

Various fuels have been used in different places and by different potters. Some-times fine brush or dried grasses were used, sometimes twigs of wood. Some groups used dried dung, which had the advantages of burning quite rapidly and evenly and of holding its shape as an ember, protecting the pottery from too rapid cooling.[1] In some cases the firing was done in a fairly deep pit, into which most of the fuel was placed right at the start with the pottery. But others used only a very shallow pit, piling the pottery and the fuel largely above ground. In either case, firings were short, and maximum heat was sometimes attained in an hour or even less.

Pit firing has the advantage of requiring no fixed structure of any kind, so that a firing can be done anywhere and with readily available fuel. The increase of heat, however, is severely limited by the open firing, which permits heat to rise without obstruction. Firing temperatures in open pits seldom exceed dull red heat,

[1] William Alexander of Colorado State University has made "artificial dung" from a mixture of sawdust, wheat flour, and bentonite, and has used it successfully in producing pit-fired black ware similar to Pueblo Indian pottery.

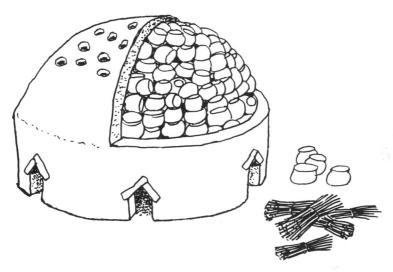

7. *A primitive kiln consisting of a low circular wall with openings for the fires. The upper part, rebuilt for each firing, is a layer of clay and straw plastered over the pots, with openings left for draft.*

or about 700° to 900° C. While this temperature is high enough to produce soft, porous earthenware, it is insufficient to fire hard, impervious pottery, or to fuse glazes. But within the limitations of low heat, early potters succeeded in producing wares that were not surpassed aesthetically by later artisans with more sophisticated firing techniques at their disposal.

Primitive pottery, although it is usually porous and easily broken, was often made with great technical ingenuity and skill. In pre-Columbian Peru, for example, the potters used a variety of hand-molding processes and clay molds in several parts and were able to fire with enough control to obtain a surprising variety of slip colors.

In pit firing, the wares were often subjected to the direct impingement of the flame, and so were discolored by black or dark areas. Careful management of the fire, however, could produce a clear, smoke-free atmosphere, resulting in well oxidized pottery.

If black pottery was desired, it could easily be produced by adding some dense fuel such as shredded dung at the end of the firing and covering the whole pit to prevent the access of air to the fuel. Such a procedure caused a buildup of carbon in the pores of the ware, making it black throughout. Both red pottery and black pottery were made from the same clay by varying the firing process. Since the firing reached only a relatively low temperature, pottery that was burnished in its raw state by rubbing with a smooth stone would retain its polish after firing. Such polished areas were often used for decorative effect.[1]

[1] For an authoritative account of primitive firing methods see A. O. Shepard, *Ceramics for the Archeologist* (Washington: Carnegie Institution of Washington, 1956) pp. 74–92.

The first stage in the development of kilns was the improvement of the pit to make it retain the heat better and to introduce the fuel in a way which would promote better circulation of heat. A simple but effective improvement of the firing pit was the introduction of holes at the lower part of the pit which would admit air for better combustion. The introduction of a little air at the bottom of the pit may yield a gain of about 100° C. A further improvement over the dug pit is the use of a low wall of clay or mud which becomes in effect a rudimentary kiln. Such a wall helps to retain the heat from the embers that accumulate toward the end of the firing. Pit kilns of this sort are still used in Spain and Mexico. Figure 7 illustrates a kiln, common to many parts of the world, which is essentially a low, circular wall with openings for fires.

The next step, a crucial one in the development of firing technique, was to introduce the fuel at the bottom of the pit or chamber, letting the flames course upward through the setting rather than relying on a bed of embers to transfer heat to the pottery.

8. *Pottery community of Sokoto, Northern Nigeria. Each kiln is 3 ft. high and 12 ft. in diameter, and when stacked has a volume of about 500 cubic ft. There are six small fireboxes fed with guinea corn stalks. The firing time is about two hours. Photo by Peter Stichbury.*

9. *Opening the kiln at Sokoto. The pottery has been covered with a layer of shards, which the potter is seen collecting. The shards are covered with a layer of dust and straw. Towards the end of the firing, when the top is getting hot, the potters try to keep the flames from breaking through by adding more dust. At the end, they heap dry grass on the top, which burns with great intensity. Photo by Peter Stichbury.*

10. *Kiln in Consuegra, Spain. The method of firing is similar to the Nigerian kiln in Figure 9. Photo by Tony Prieto.*

Primitive kilns of the Near East illustrate this next stage of kiln design. The kilns still in operation in Iraq, North Africa, and Crete are no doubt very similar to those developed in Ancient Egypt and Mesopotamia, the first true ceramic kilns.[1]

The form of the kiln was essentially a cylinder, open at the top, with an entrance tunnel for the fire provided at the bottom, as shown in Figure 11. The floor or platform on which the ware was set was perforated with holes to let the fire pass

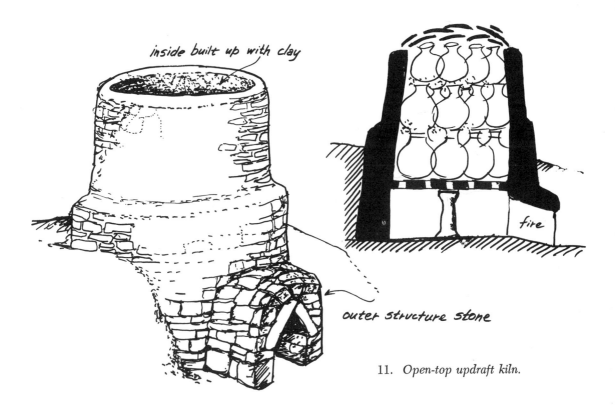

inside built up with clay

outer structure stone

11. *Open-top updraft kiln.*

upward. In some cases this floor was built of large fired clay bars wedged across the cylinder, with clay partially filling in the space between the bars. The ware to be fired was piled into the cylindrical chamber. The fire was built in the entrance, and the flame and hot gases from the fire passed upward through the ware, escaping from the top. The top of the kiln could be partially closed off by a loose thatch-

[1] For a detailed study of kilns and pottery methods in Cyprus, Crete, and Mycenae, see Roland Hampe and Adam Winter, *Bei Töpfern und Töpferinnen in Kreta, Messenien, und Zypern* (Mainz: Verlag des Römisch-Germanischen Zentralmuseums Mainz, 1962, In Kommission Bei Rudolf Habelt Verlag, Bonn.)

12.   Open-top updraft kiln in Margueritas, Crete. The potter is making five large jars, each of which is turned on its own wheel. The potter works on each piece in turn, while the others stiffen in the sun.

13.   Updraft kiln in Crete. The single firemouth is below ground level.

14. *Large updraft kiln at Bab Tisra, Morocco. The walls of the cylindrical structure are heavily buttressed. Photo by Nan Sugar, courtesy of* Craft Horizons.

ing of broken pottery or tiles. This design represents a great advance over the pit fire, incorporating all the elements of the kiln as we know it today: a fireplace or mouth in which fuel can be burned and heat generated; a chamber in which the ware is placed and which will retain heat; and a flue or exit from which the hot gases can escape, thus creating a draft that pulls air into the firemouth and moves the heat upward through the kiln. Although there was much room for improvement in the design, this arrangement of elements furnished the prototype for most ceramic kilns used in the Mediterranean area and in Europe down to modern times.[1]

Early kilns in Egypt, Asia Minor and the Mediterranean area were made from sandy adobe brick, fired brick, or from sandstone. The walls of the kilns were laid up with clay, and often earth was piled up around the structure for better heat retention and support. The kilns were often constructed against a hill or bank. At this stage, the kiln became a fixed structure, and could withstand numerous firings. Early kilns in the Mediterranean area were loaded from the top. The pottery

[1] According to Isabelle Chang in *Chinese Cooking Made Easy* (Liveright, 1959), kilns of this general type have been unearthed near Chengchow, China. Since they are from the Shang period, they may antedate the bank or climbing chamber kiln.

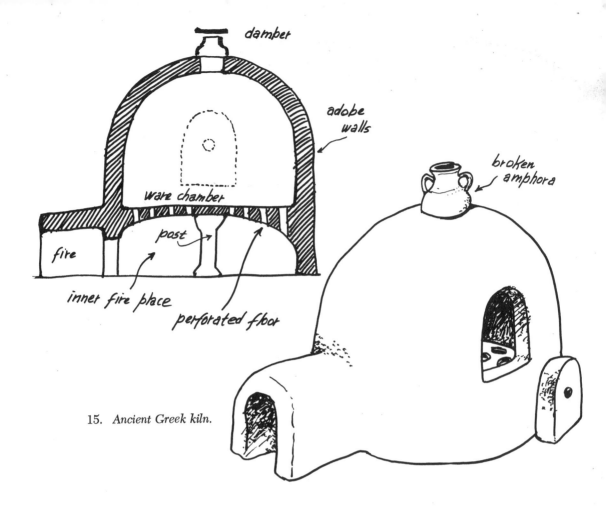

15. *Ancient Greek kiln.*

16. *Greek kiln as depicted on an ancient Corinthian pinax. The potter is raking the coals from the firemouth of the kiln. The kiln door with its spy hole and the vent at the top of the kiln are clearly indicated.* From Techniques of Painted Attic Pottery *by Joseph V. Noble (New York: Watson-Guptill, 1965).*

was piled together in stacks or bungs, leaving sufficient passage for the flames. Toward the top, a layer of broken shards was placed over the pots, overlapping like loose shingles to retain the heat. The firemouth was large enough to contain a sizable fire, with bricks or stones placed in it to form a grate and to enable air to reach the burning fuel. Brush, reeds, small twigs or branches, or split wood was used for fuel. With dry brush a fiercely hot flame could be generated in the firemouth, producing a rapid buildup of temperature in the chamber.

The advantages of a simple updraft kiln of this type are obvious. The fire can be controlled and may vary from a low smoldering fire at the beginning to a fiercely hot blaze at the height of the firing. The hot gases and flame from the fire effectively circulate heat directly to the ware. The walls of the kiln retain the heat, and as the surfaces of the walls become red hot they reflect heat back into the kiln. The top of the kiln can be covered during the firing, to retain heat but allow the escape of sufficient hot gases to create a draft.

17. *Ancient Corinthian pinax, showing the interior of the kiln. The figure at the left is a restoration by R. M. Cook. The vases in the kiln are clearly shown, but are probably in a more helter-skelter arrangement than they would have been in an actual firing. The perforated floor is shown with its supporting post below. The embers of the fire are represented with dots. Near the top of the kiln, two draw trials are shown, both with holes in them to enable the potter to hook them out with a rod. From* Techniques of Painted Attic Pottery *by Joseph V. Noble.*

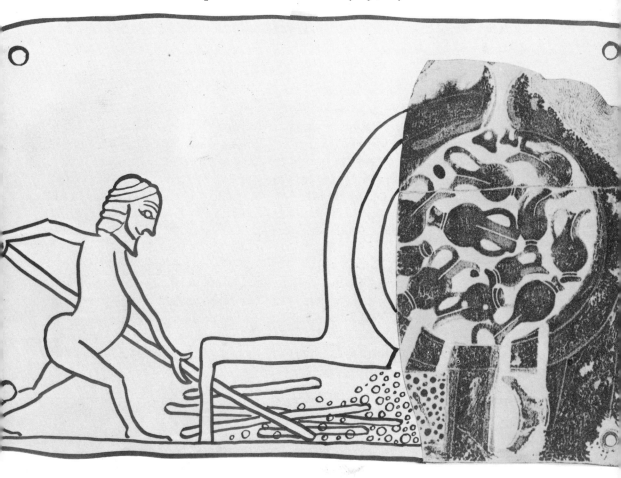

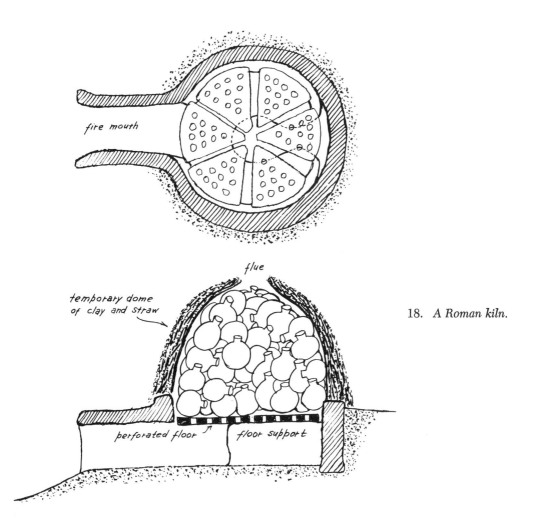

fire mouth

temporary dome
of clay and straw

flue

perforated floor   floor support

18. *A Roman kiln.*

We know from the ceramic wares produced in Egypt, Mesopotamia, Crete, and the Aegean areas that primitive, open-topped, updraft kilns reached 900° C., and in some cases were fired perhaps as high as 1050° C. This relatively high temperature, together with a degree of control over the advance of heat, enabled the improvement of pottery and the development of ceramic glazes. Once this basic updraft kiln was perfected, little further improvement was made in kiln design in the Mediterranean area and in Europe until comparatively recent times.

The design of kilns used in ancient Greece is quite certainly known from depictions on ancient pottery. With their knowledge of how to construct a dome, the Greeks built their kilns in the shape of a beehive, as shown in Figure 15. The fire was introduced into a small tunnel leading into the chamber. The draft was controlled by opening and closing a hole at the top. From ancient drawings we can be certain that the kiln had a door, a hearth on which the pottery was probably placed, and a space below for combustion. The Greek kiln was probably made of fired bricks or adobe. Judging from the perfection of finished Greek pottery, with its refinement of surface decoration, we can be sure that the kilns were under good control and could be made to oxidize or reduce as desired. Greek kilns were probably not large, perhaps no more than six feet in diameter.[1]

Most of our information on Roman kilns comes from archeological studies in the British Isles. Roman legions stationed in England maintained sizable ceramic plants for the production of brick, pottery, and tile. The remains of such kilns have been found at Holt in Denbighshire. Here a factory complex has been excavated which consists of seven or more large kilns. These kilns in essence were sizable perforated clay floors with a space underneath in which the fires were built. The wares to be fired were evidently arranged on these floors and were mudded over to form a temporary "scove" kiln which would retain the heat.

Many smaller Roman kilns have been excavated at various sites in England. Most of these are of the general type illustrated in Figure 18. It will be seen that the design is not unlike the Greek kiln except that the ware itself was set in a temporary chamber rebuilt for each firing. The fire was built in a firemouth which led into a combustion chamber below the kiln proper. The ware was placed on perforated clay floor tiles or on clay bars, supported in part on a pedestal extending into the combustion chamber from the back. The raw pots were piled up on this floor in a beehive shape, and over the pile of pots several layers of clay and straw were plastered, leaving enough openings at the top for the escape of the hot gases from the fire. The kilns were four to six feet in diameter, and the firemouth was usually eighteen to twenty-four inches across.[2]

---

[1] Joseph V. Noble, in *The Techniques of Painted Attic Pottery* (New York: Watson-Gupthill, 1965) gives a definitive account of the techniques of forming, decorating, and firing practiced by the ancient Greeks. Also in this book is a translation of the poem "Kiln," attributed to Homer.

[2] For an excellent study of Roman kilns see Philip Corder, "The Structure of Romano-British Kilns," *Archeological Journal*, Vol. MXIV, 1957, pp. 10–27.

2

Kilns of the Orient

ONE OF THE MOST FASCINATING aspects of the history of ceramics is the development of kilns in the Orient. At an early date, the kilns in use in China, Korea, and Japan were superior to any in the rest of the world until comparatively recent times. The high achievements of the Oriental potters were made possible to a considerable extent by their possession of well constructed, efficient kilns in which a relatively exacting control of temperature and atmosphere was attainable. The development of porcelain depended on the attainment of very high firing temperatures. Such temperatures were possible in Oriental style kilns, but were completely out of reach in the more primitive kilns used in the West.

Ceramic art in China is of such antiquity that the design of the earliest kilns used can never be known. It is certain, however, that by about 1000 B.C. Chinese potters were making wares that were fired above 1100°C., and we can infer the existence at about this period of a kiln that would reach temperatures higher than any previously attained in other parts of the world. One possible clue to the design of the earliest types of kilns in the Orient is the surviving remains of cave or bank kilns in Japan. These kilns were used in Japan from about the eighth century to the thirteenth century, and enough archeological remnants of them still exist to enable us to reconstruct their original form and method of operation. Ruins of such kilns have been found near Seto, where they were used for the production of the Sue pottery and for firing early Seto stoneware. Other cave kilns have been found near Fukui, where the Echizen style of pottery was made. These cave kilns must have been copied from similar kilns on the mainland of Asia; the knowledge of building and firing them probably came from Korea. It is possible that these Japanese kilns represent a type which was used for the first high-fired stoneware of China.

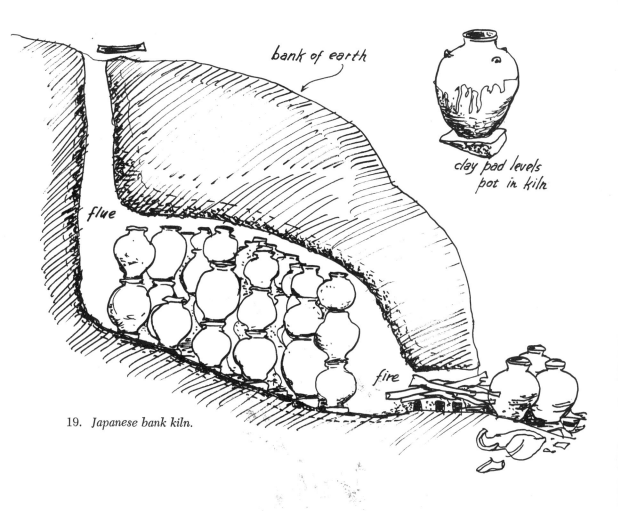

bank of earth

clay pad levels
pot in kiln

flue

fire

19. *Japanese bank kiln.*

The Japanese cave kiln was made by digging a cave into a bank, as shown in Figure 19. By present day standards, the kilns were not large. The main chamber was about four or five feet across, three feet high, and ten or twelve feet long. The cave sloped at an angle of about 30°. The entrance to the cave was just large enough for a man to crawl through. At the back, a flue hole was cut, leading to ground level above. The kiln was located in an area of sandy soil with considerable clay in it. Soil containing rock would not be sufficiently stable when heated. The kiln was set by crawling in through the opening with the pots, which were set on the sloping floor on wedge-shaped pads of clay to make the pieces stand upright. Pieces were stacked one on the other, with no shelves or saggers. The fire was built in the entrance. Flames traveled upward through the ware, and out the flue. After numerous firings, the inside of the kiln became fired, and the hard crust of burned soil formed a tough and relatively permanent lining for the cave.

These early cave kilns of Japan may seem crude and rudimentary but beautiful high-fired stoneware was produced in them. They represented an advance in design over the simple updraft kiln of the Near East. Since the kiln was completely inclosed and backed up with earth, it retained the heat well. Furthermore, the heat

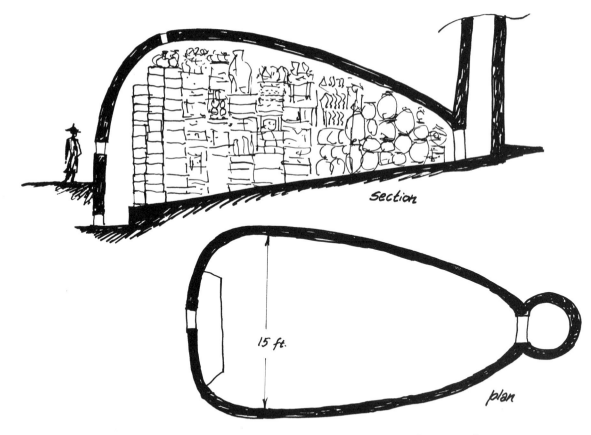

section

15 ft.

plan

20. *A Chinese kiln of the type used at Ching-tê-chên for firing porcelain.*

was forced into a crossdraft path, instead of sweeping directly upwards, and thus was transmitted more efficiently to the ware. The flue hole was only large enough to produce sufficient draft, and could be closed off for adjustment. From the cave kiln it was only one step to the downdraft kiln developed in China.

Figure 20 shows the design of a modern Chinese kiln of the type used at Ching-tê-chên, ancient center of porcelain production. Its shape is essentially the same as the cave kiln. The structure is roofed over with a dome, somewhat in the shape of a beehive. The cross section of the kiln diminishes toward the back and the opening into the chimney is at floor level.[1] The floor slants upward somewhat. Ware is set in the kiln in such a way as to baffle the heat upward toward the dome. The flames then pass across and down through the setting to the flue. The rather indirect circulation through the kiln favors an efficient exchange of heat to the

---

[1] In designing a kiln which had a diminishing cross section towards the flue, the Chinese apparently hit upon a principle which promoted even temperature. The hot gases as they passed through the constricted rear of the kiln traveled with increased velocity and therefore more heat was transmitted to that part of the setting by convection than would be the case in a rectangular kiln. See Part II, Section 3 below on heat transfer.

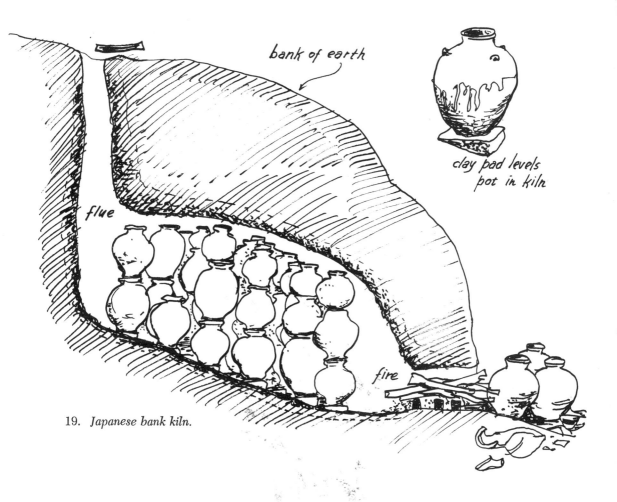

bank of earth

clay pad levels
pot in kiln

flue

fire

19. *Japanese bank kiln.*

The Japanese cave kiln was made by digging a cave into a bank, as shown in Figure 19. By present day standards, the kilns were not large. The main chamber was about four or five feet across, three feet high, and ten or twelve feet long. The cave sloped at an angle of about 30°. The entrance to the cave was just large enough for a man to crawl through. At the back, a flue hole was cut, leading to ground level above. The kiln was located in an area of sandy soil with considerable clay in it. Soil containing rock would not be sufficiently stable when heated. The kiln was set by crawling in through the opening with the pots, which were set on the sloping floor on wedge-shaped pads of clay to make the pieces stand upright. Pieces were stacked one on the other, with no shelves or saggers. The fire was built in the entrance. Flames traveled upward through the ware, and out the flue. After numerous firings, the inside of the kiln became fired, and the hard crust of burned soil formed a tough and relatively permanent lining for the cave.

These early cave kilns of Japan may seem crude and rudimentary but beautiful high-fired stoneware was produced in them. They represented an advance in design over the simple updraft kiln of the Near East. Since the kiln was completely inclosed and backed up with earth, it retained the heat well. Furthermore, the heat

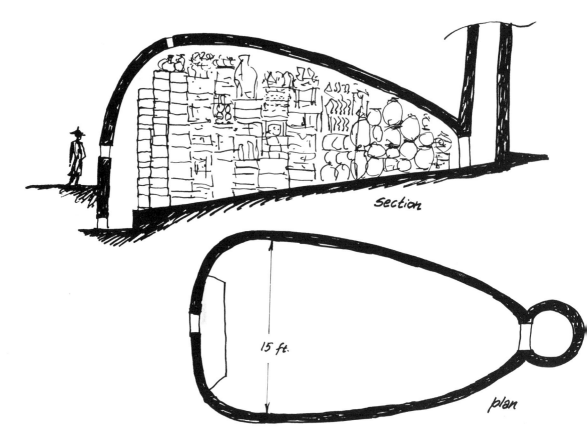

Section

15 ft.

plan

20. *A Chinese kiln of the type used at Ching-tê-chên for firing porcelain.*

was forced into a crossdraft path, instead of sweeping directly upwards, and thus was transmitted more efficiently to the ware. The flue hole was only large enough to produce sufficient draft, and could be closed off for adjustment. From the cave kiln it was only one step to the downdraft kiln developed in China.

Figure 20 shows the design of a modern Chinese kiln of the type used at Ching-tê-chên, ancient center of porcelain production. Its shape is essentially the same as the cave kiln. The structure is roofed over with a dome, somewhat in the shape of a beehive. The cross section of the kiln diminishes toward the back and the opening into the chimney is at floor level.[1] The floor slants upward somewhat. Ware is set in the kiln in such a way as to baffle the heat upward toward the dome. The flames then pass across and down through the setting to the flue. The rather indirect circulation through the kiln favors an efficient exchange of heat to the

[1] In designing a kiln which had a diminishing cross section towards the flue, the Chinese apparently hit upon a principle which promoted even temperature. The hot gases as they passed through the constricted rear of the kiln traveled with increased velocity and therefore more heat was transmitted to that part of the setting by convection than would be the case in a rectangular kiln. See Part II, Section 3 below on heat transfer.

ware. Kilns of this general type were probably in use in China by the beginning of the Christian era, and perhaps earlier.

The Chinese not only were clever designers and builders of kilns, but they also had good refractory materials to work with. Fireclays and kaolins are quite common in China and were widely used for kilns, whereas in Europe and the Near East, bricks of ordinary red clay were used. The more refractory materials were able to withstand high firing temperatures. In some Chinese kilns blocks of unfired clay were used, but more commonly, regular bricks, made and fired for the purpose, were employed.

The multi-chambered kiln as it developed in China was a near perfect design. Several chambers were linked together on a sloping site, through which the heat passed from one to the next, as shown in Figure 21. This design makes use of downdraft circulation, with the exhaust heat of each chamber being utilized for warming up the next. When all the chambers are set with ware and the doors bricked in, a fire is started in the main firemouth. This is a domed enclosure with a grate for holding the fuel and passages to admit air. The fire is kept low at first

21. *An Oriental chamber kiln.*

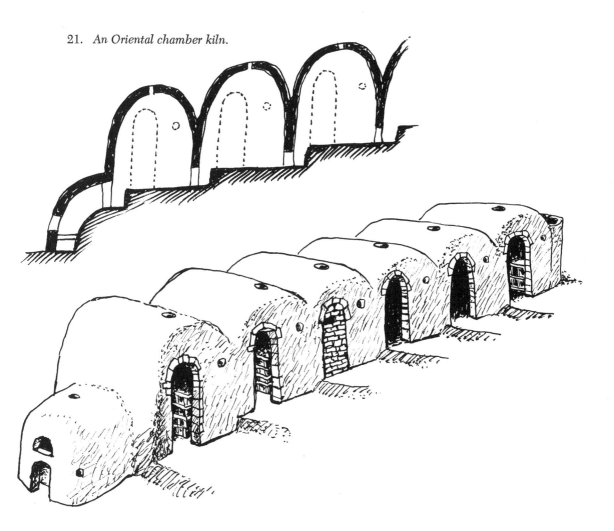

22. *A model of a Japanése chamber kiln. The model represents a type of kiln formerly used in the Seto region. There are three separate firemouths, and another large firing chamber built below the first ware chamber. This kiln was larger than any now in use in Japan. Model in the Municipal Historical Museum, Seto, Japan.*

23. *Kiln in Shigaraki, Japan. The Shigaraki kilns have an unusually steep slope.*

24. *Japanese chamber kiln.*

to dry out the ware, then gradually increased until a temperature of 1250° C. or more is reached. The heat from the firemouth warms the whole kiln and a strong draft develops in the ascending chambers. When maximum heat is reached in the firemouth, the first chamber will have reached red heat or more throughout. Fuel is then fed into the first chamber through openings in the door. No special grate is provided here, but the wood burns rapidly because the air for combustion is preheated as it passes through the main firemouth. When the temperature in the first chamber rises to the desired degree, firing begins in the second chamber. Preheated air reaches this chamber from the now cooling first chamber. Thus the firing proceeds up the slope. When the last chamber is reached, little, if any, additional fuel is required.

The chambered kiln has some admirable design features. Architecturally, the structure is quite self-supporting. Since each chamber serves as a buttress for the next, no external bracing is necessary. When heated, the expanding domes rise without undue strain on any part of the kiln. The walls of the kiln are fairly thin and without insulation, in contrast to Japanese kiln walls which are usually about eight inches thick and made of hard firebrick. Since the firing is quite rapid, the

25. *Shoji Hamada's kiln at Mashiko, Japan.*

lack of insulation is not a great disadvantage. The heat hardly has time to work itself through the walls.

The generous size of the main firemouth permits the rapid burning of a large quantity of fuel and a consequent rapid buildup of heat. The firing spaces within the chambers themselves also have ample room for the combustion of fuel. This, together with the large amount of air that is drawn in by the ascending gases in the entire kiln, enables the rapid release of great quantities of heat.

In each chamber, the forward wall of pottery or saggers is arranged in such a way as to deflect the heat upwards. The flame and hot gases then pass downward through the setting and through the passages to the next chamber. Considerable control of the temperature in various parts of the chamber is possible through the arrangement of the setting.

Usually provided at the top of each chamber are one or more blow holes, which may be opened during the firing to permit some of the flame to escape at that point. The upward slope of the kiln, inducing the rise through the chambers of a large volume of hot gases, makes a chimney unnecessary at the last chamber.

Chamber kilns in China are large, often having an interior height of 15 feet and

26. *Kiln at Ryomonji, in southern Japan. The kiln shed is roofed with cypress bark.*

up to eight chambers. Such kilns hold many thousands of pots. Japanese kilns are usually smaller, but some have an interior height of 6 feet.

One disadvantage of the sloping chamber kiln is the tendency toward rapid cooling. All the air for combustion passes through chambers that are cooling, and while this increases efficiency by heating the air, it takes heat from the ware in the early stages of cooling. The last chamber, however, if thoroughly closed up after firing, will cool slowly.

Figure 27 is a chamber kiln at Tehwa in the province of Fukien in South China. The drawing is based on data obtained by Willard J. Sutton in 1935. The kiln consists of six chambers of very large size. Each chamber is 20 feet deep, ten feet wide, and 15 feet high. The floor of each chamber is divided into five steps on which the rows of saggers are set. The domes are somewhat pointed and are laid with bricks set in a herringbone pattern. The walls of the kiln are approximately two feet thick at the bottom, reinforced and buttressed with rock on the outside. Doors are provided at both sides of each chamber, but the doors are quite low, just a bit over five feet high.

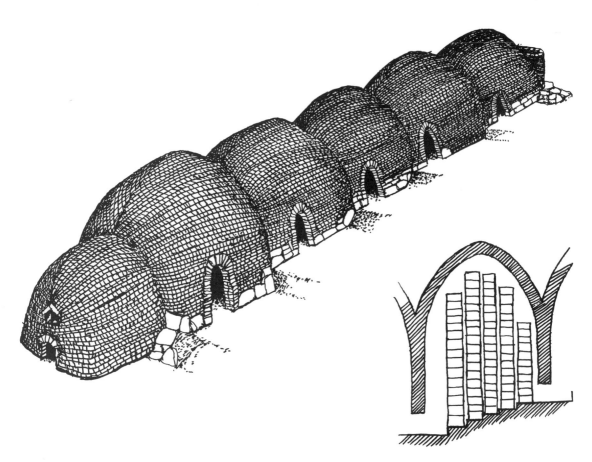

27.   *Large chamber kiln for porcelain at Tewah, Fukien Province, China. Drawing based on data supplied by Dr. W. J. Sutton.*

28.   *A Korean "split bamboo" kiln.*

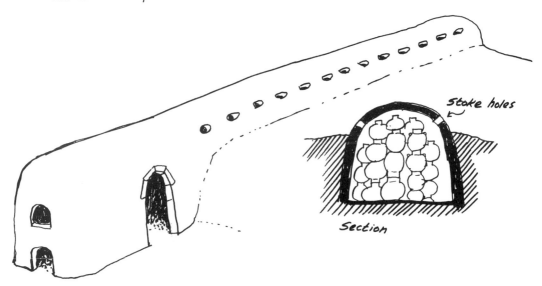

29. *Korean potters preparing for a firing.*

These kilns were constructed of very large firebrick, made locally. The kilns at Tehwa were used for porcelain manufacture, and were fired to approximately cone 14 in a neutral or reducing atmosphere. Each chamber was fired for about 24 hours, and the whole firing operation extended over a week's time. It is not known whether these Tehwa kilns are still in production.

The Korean kiln, Figure 28, is also built on a slope, but is not divided into separate chambers. It may be a surviving type which had been in use earlier in China, or it may be a local Korean development.[1] The kiln is essentially a long tube, partially buried in the earth and set on a slope of about 25°. It has been called the "split bamboo" kiln because of its half-buried form. The chamber may be six feet high inside and 100 feet or more in length. It is probable that this style of kiln, still in use, is similar to those in use during the best years of Korean pottery, from about 1000 A.D. to the end of the Yi Dynasty in 1910.

In the Korean system of firing, there were no chambers or separations in the long kiln. Each part is fired by stoking through holes in the top of the kiln. These stoking

[1] Dr. Sutton reports seeing kilns in Fukien province, China, which had very little dividing wall between chambers. These kilns may be surviving examples of the prototype of the Korean kiln.

30. *A Korean kiln. Photo by Young Suk Kim.*

31. *A Korean kiln. Photo by Young Suk Kim.*

holes are located four or five feet apart on both sides of the kiln. At the start, a fire in the main firemouth brings the lower part of the kiln up to the desired temperature. Then each pair of stoke holes is plied with wood, and the zone of highest heat travels up the kiln. No special grate is provided below the stoke holes; the wood is just tossed in to burn among the rows of pottery. Needless to say, some of the pots are broken in the process. Since the air coming from finished sections is hot, combustion is quick and intense, and the temperature of the zone being fired rises very rapidly.

32. *Stoke holes at the top of a Korean kiln. The clay plugs are removed when fuel is being fed into the kiln. Photo by Young Suk Kim.*

The Korean kiln must be considered more primitive in design than the chambered sloping kiln of China and Japan, but it operates with fair efficiency. It is loaded by entering either through the firemouth or through an opening in the side of the kiln just above the firemouth. The upward slope of the large chamber gives a powerful draft. Once brought up to red heat over most of its length, it consumes fuel at a rate sufficient for a rapid rise of temperature. Exact control over temperature and atmosphere, however, is not possible in a kiln of this type. During the firing, two men work on either side of the kiln, stoking wood into opposite stoke holes. Rather long poles of wood are used which burn crosswise in the kiln between tiers of pots. Temperature is gauged by color alone, and the effect of stoking is to raise one rather short section of the kiln to the desired heat. Then the stoking proceeds to the next pair of holes. Korean kilns of this type are now used almost exclusively to fire *kimchi* jars, used by the Korean householder for pickling.

An interesting variation of the Korean style kiln is the type used in Japan at the village of Tachikui, Hyōgo prefecture, for the production of Tamba wares. About twenty of these kilns are still in operation. The original design was probably established by immigrant Korean potters about 1600 A.D. The Tachikui kilns are about 150 feet long, and are built on the hillside with an upward slope of about 30°. Like the Korean kiln, the structure is essentially a long tube, partially buried in the earth as shown in Figure 33. The kilns are made of handmade refractory brick laid with considerable clay mortar to form the barrel vault. The cross section of the kiln is rather small—4½ feet wide and about 3 feet high. Spaced along the kiln are seven or eight doors, and the kiln bulges out a bit at the doors to form a wider interior space. At these points, some piers from floor to arch help support the structure, but there is no division into separate chambers. Between doors there are

33. *A Tamba kiln, Japan.*

cross section
at door

34.   A Tamba kiln at Tachikui, Japan.

35.   A Tamba kiln at Tachikui, Japan.

36. *Tamba kiln. The potter is poking the fire with an iron rod.*

ten or more pairs of stoke holes. At the lower end of the kiln an igloo-shaped chamber serves as main firemouth. The whole kiln, smeared with clay on the outside, cracked, and darkened with soot, has a very organic form, more like a natural object than something man-made. Large flat rocks are laid at the base of the kiln walls to buttress the arch.

The kiln is loaded through the doors, but workers must crawl back into the areas between doors, dragging pots with them in baskets. The fire is started in the main firemouth and continued there for a long period, 40 hours or more, at which point the lower end of the kiln has reached red heat, and a powerful draft is pushing up the long tube. Stoking is then commenced at the pairs of side holes, and each zone is brought to about 1250° C. Top temperatures are maintained only briefly, and cooling is very rapid. In fact, the first doors at the lower end of the kiln are sometimes opened while the upper part of the kiln is still firing. 200 bundles of wood are required for the initial warmup through the main firemouth, and 20 to 25 bundles are consumed in each section. (A bundle, as made up in Japan, contains about 8 lbs. of wood.) About 1½ tons of wood are used for a firing, not an excessive quantity, considering the large capacity of the kiln, over 1000 cubic feet.

Chambered kilns were built in Japan as early as 1600 A.D., and were no doubt designed and constructed at first by Koreans. There are some variations in different localities, but in general, Japanese kilns are similar to Chinese, though usually smaller. Japanese kilns are built on a slope of about 20°, and sometimes, when no hill is available, an artificial one is created by building a mound of dirt and rock. The kiln is built directly on the ground. Hard firebricks are used. Most Japanese firebricks are not standardized in size and are generally more square in shape than our standard brick. The wall of the kiln is usually only one brick thick, about 7 to 9 inches, and no insulation is used except for a plastering of clay on the outside. Japanese kiln masons use a great deal of mortar, which is made up as a stiff paste of

37. *Firing the Tamba kiln. The stoke hole plug is lifted out with a stick.*

38. *Unstacking the Tamba kiln.*

fireclay and grog. Rubble construction is often used for part or even the whole of
the kiln. These kilns are constructed almost predominantly by modeling, with a
great deal of clay used between brick fragments. The broken bits of brick are
usually saved when a kiln is torn down, and are incorporated into the new kiln.
Temporary forms to hold the domes during construction are made from bent strips
of bamboo lashed together. The kilns are rather loosely constructed, at least by our
standards of masonry, but they are durable and sound. Possibly the rather casual
bricklaying makes the kiln more adaptable to the expansion and contraction of
heating and cooling. The Japanese say that cracks in the domes of the kiln,
resembling the designs on a turtle's shell, indicate that it was well built.

Figure 198 shows the dimensions of a small Japanese chambered kiln. Larger
kilns are of essentially the same design, except for the addition of more chambers,
and the addition of doors at both ends of the chambers instead of at one side only.
No external bracing is used, since the domes buttress each other.

To fire, each chamber is set with a wall of saggers facing the combustion zone.
These saggers, which in effect are a deflection or bag wall, are placed close
together. Chinks may be left near the bottom, however, to allow some flame to

cross directly through the bottom part of the chamber. The saggers are piled up to within about 18 inches of the crown of the kiln, and sometimes rows of pots are put on top of the saggers. Flashing may be severe at this point. The rest of the setting is made up of shelves and posts, some of which are left in place from one firing to the next. The settings are usually quite loose to permit easy circulation, with a great deal of the space taken up by the saggers and other kiln furniture.

Some Japanese kilns are used by one potter only, while others, especially those in the cities, are used by groups. The owners of the kiln rent out space, charging in accordance with the demand for various parts of the different chambers. Some kilns operate partly reducing, partly oxidizing, and the usual temperature range is from cone 8 to cone 11. Many potters fire all their wares in communal kilns, often transporting the pottery to be fired for miles through the city streets. Other potters make part of their income by renting out space in their kilns to others not fortunate enough to own a kiln. Large kilns of six chambers are fired in about six days' time.

Unfortunately, the chambered wood-fired kiln is disappearing in Japan, not so much because of its inefficiency, but because of the high cost of wood. The numerous kilns in the city of Kyoto create an air pollution problem, and a city ordinance has prohibited the construction of new ones.

3

European and
Modern Kilns

IN THE MEDITERRANEAN AREA no fundamental improve-
ment was made in kilns from antiquity until fairly recent times. Islamic potters
from Persia to Spain used a kiln which was essentially a round or square chamber,
roofed over with a barrel vault or dome, and heated with wood burning fireboxes
arranged at the lower part of the chamber. Hot gases escaped through holes in the
crown after ascending through the ware. Even if very high temperatures could
have been reached with the fuel burning and draft arrangement, the materials of
the walls and crown were not sufficiently refractory to resist them.

Figure 39 shows a kiln used in Spain in the Hispano-Moorish period. It is probably
very similar in design to kilns used in Persia, Iraq, and Egypt during the best
periods of Islamic pottery.[1] The kiln is solidly constructed with strong buttressing
to support the arch, and ample firebox area is provided. One curious feature of this
design is the provision of a shelf at the rear of the main fireplace on which the ware
was placed for bisque firing. Since the draft of the kiln was upwards, only radiant
heat warmed this part of the kiln, and the temperature here was lower than in the
upper chamber. The relatively large chamber for combustion permitted the burning of bulky bundles of brush or small wood. Kilns of this type certainly operated
with creditable efficiency and control, as attested by the beautiful glazed wares
that were fired in them. Unevenness of temperature must have been a problem,
however, and it is hard to see how pots in the upper part of the kiln could have
reached temperatures anywhere near that of the bottom of the ware chamber.

---

[1] For an excellent description of the methods of Islamic potters, see Hans E. Wulff, *The Traditional
Crafts of Persia*, Cambridge, Mass.: M.I.T. Press, 1966.

flue holes

door

bisque

fire

39. *Medieval Spanish kiln.*

Figure 40 shows an Italian kiln of the 16th century as depicted in a drawing by Piccolpasso. Piccolpasso, who wrote the first "how-to-do-it" book on pottery,[1] is our best source of information on the pottery methods of the time, and is recommended to readers who are interested in the development of the craft. The Italian kiln is somewhat similar to the Spanish kiln. It is composed of two chambers, a fireplace or combustion space below, and a chamber for the ware above. Arches support the floor of the ware chamber. Flames travel upward through holes in this floor and out through holes in the arched ceiling above. The updraft arrangement must have made the temperature near the floor considerably higher than that of the upper part of the chamber, and perhaps bisque ware was placed at the top. The firebox seems unnecessarily large. We are not sure what kinds of bricks were used, but probably they were just common red bricks. European earthenware production from Roman times down to the present has been fired in simple updraft kilns no different in basic design from the early Italian and Spanish kilns illustrated. Wood or brush was the usual fuel, and the firing temperature seldom exceeded about 1000° C. There were, of course, many local variations of design and firing methods.

Luster kilns were used by the Persian, Spanish, and later by the Italian potters to fire metallic luster surfaces on glazed pottery. Figure 41 illustrates a luster kiln from the Medieval Spanish period. It is quite small, measuring only a few feet across. Fuel is burned in the firebox below, and flame rises into the ware chamber through holes in the center and at the corners of the floor of the ware chamber.

[1] Cipriano Piccolpasso, *The Three Books of the Potter's Art.* (London: Victoria & Albert Museum, 1934).

o sin qui
fornato
empre di
gli accide
nescici
i fa

atto & gia la fornace comincie
no so che del chiaro allora sabbiasi

40. Renaissance Italian kiln. Drawings by Piccolpasso.

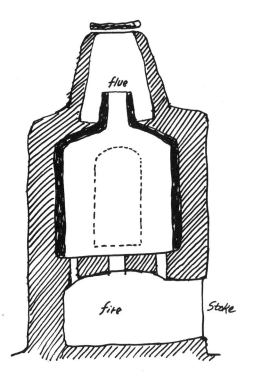

41. *Medieval Spanish luster kiln.*

The flue at the top vents into a hovel type chimney. The luster kiln was fired with a heavily reducing atmosphere, and its design differed from the regular pottery kiln mainly in the size of the flue. A similar luster kiln illustrated in Piccolpasso's book is also a small updraft oven, but it incorporates a perforated muffle in which the ware is placed, and has no permanent top, the kiln being closed over at the top by chips or fragments of broken pottery. It was loaded from the top.[1]

Great advances in kiln design and construction were made in Europe during the Industrial Revolution, and by about 1800, kilns were in service in European factories which were the equal of Chinese kilns. Improved refractories, better arrangements for the circulation of heat, and the introduction of coal for fuel enabled the attainment of higher temperatures.

Porcelain was first made in Europe in 1710 by Boettger in Germany, and no small part of his achievement was the development of a small kiln which would reach the necessary 1300° C., an unheard of temperature among European potters of the day. Boettger and his followers used bricks made of refractory clay, and introduced well designed fireboxes with cast iron grate bars. The kiln was elongated upwards into a bottle shape with a chimney at the top. This greatly increased the draft and fuel burning capacity. Coke and coal were used for fuel, and with a

---

[1] Piccolpasso, *op. cit.*

strong draft through an open firebox and grate, sufficient heat could be released for very high temperatures.[1]

Figure 42 illustrates a type of kiln which was widely used in various parts of Europe for pottery production. It is a round structure with several fireplaces at the

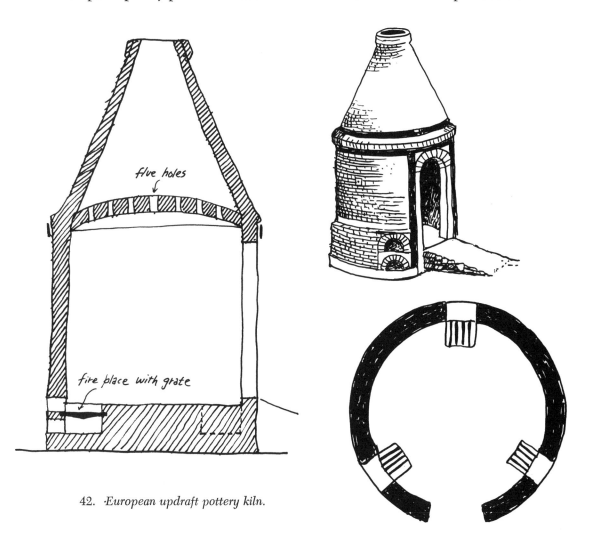

flue holes

fire place with grate

42. ·*European updraft pottery kiln.*

bottom. The flames travel upwards through the setting and through holes in the crown, the general plan being not too different from the kiln of Piccolpasso.

[1] A great deal of secrecy surrounded the early manufacture of porcelain and exact data on the early kilns is lacking. In Diderot's *Encyclopedia,* the article on porcelain is so inaccurate as to be misleading, probably because its author had no way of determining exactly how porcelain was made, and could only speculate.

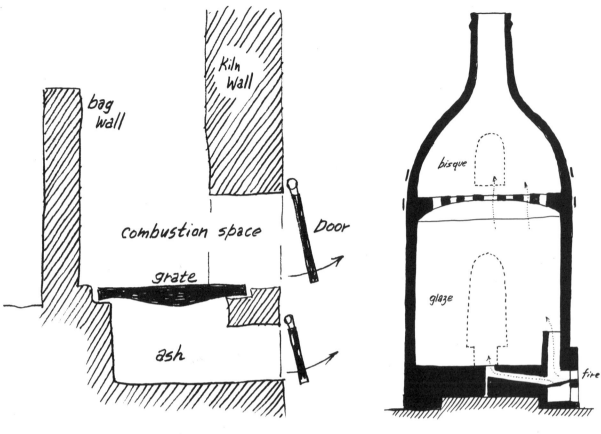

43. *Grate for burning coal.*

44. *Bottle kiln.*

However, a chimney has been constructed over the kiln, and the stronger draft which this creates makes for higher temperatures and increased efficiency.

The development of cast iron grates for fuel burning brought about a considerable improvement. Figure 43 shows a schematic design of a fireplace and grate. The coal or wood is held on the iron bars, and air for combustion enters from below. Ashes drop through the grate and are collected below, where they can be raked out from time to time. This arrangement is similar to the disposition of elements in any coal burning furnace or stove. It brings the air to all surfaces of the fuel.

The updraft pottery kiln grew to become a high, bottle-shaped kiln with a bisque chamber above, as shown in Figure 44. In this design, part of the flame is diverted to the center of the kiln through passages under the floor, while the rest of the flame rises directly upward behind low bag walls. This distribution of flame spreads the heat more evenly over the cross section of the kiln. The bisque chamber is entered through a door which usually coincides with the second story of the pottery factory. Careful management of the fires and a long firing cycle gave fairly even temperatures in the lower chamber. This type of kiln was widely used for earthenware and porcelain manufacture. Ware was set in saggers to protect it from the direct impingement of flame.

One disadvantage of the bottle-shaped kiln was the stress of the heavy upper chamber and chimney on the lower chamber, necessitating thick wall sections and heavy external bracing of chains or iron bands. The hovel kiln, as shown in Figure 45 has a chimney or "hovel" constructed outside the main part of the kiln and not resting on it. This structure was cheaper to build than the bottle kiln, and was easier to keep in repair. Sometimes the hovel was built large enough to cover the whole kiln like a hat, and the men tending the fires worked within the hovel.

Round updraft kilns were substantially built, with walls 18 inches thick or more. For porcelain production the interior was made of firebrick, but for earthenware the kilns were constructed of a good grade of red or buff brick, and no insulation was used. Doors, or "wickets," were bricked in each time.

Beginning with the Industrial Revolution and especially during the nineteenth century, much work was done in the improvement of kilns. The motivation was, of course, economic. Better kilns produced more uniform products and consumed less fuel. Industrialization also made larger kilns necessary, both for pottery production and for the production of heavy clay products such as brick and tile.

45. *Hovel kiln.*

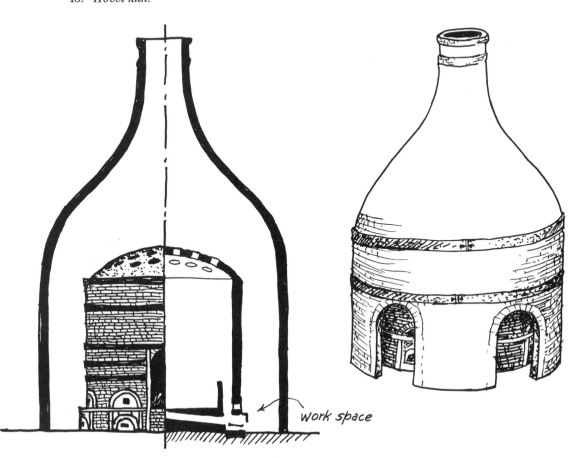

work space

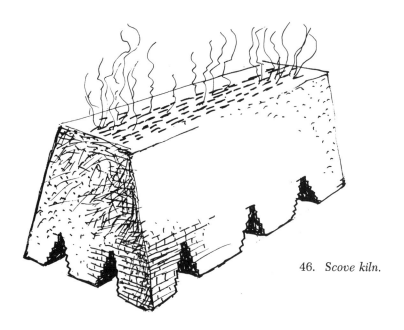

46. *Scove kiln.*

Early brick kilns in Europe were primitive structures, often built without any roof. Figure 46 shows a "scove" kiln for firing bricks. Actually, it is not a kiln but a method of firing bricks without a kiln. The raw bricks are piled up in a manner which provides fireplaces at the base of the structure and passageways for flame leading from the fires to the top. The outside of the pile is plastered over with clay mixed with straw, with chinks left at the top for escape of the hot gases. Coal fires

47. *Cassel kiln.*

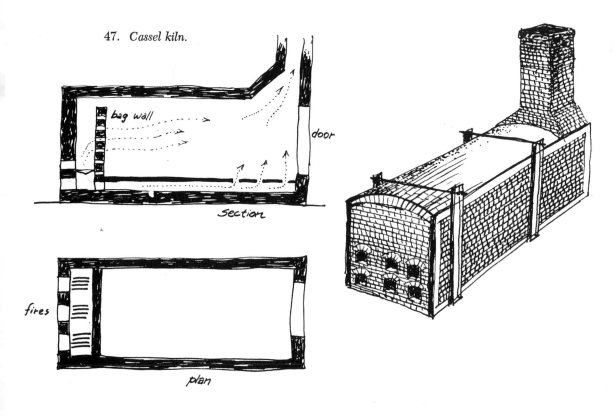

bag wall

door

Section

fires

plan

are started, and the whole interior becomes red hot. Bricks near the fires tend to become overfired, and those at the outside are underfired. These are placed in the next firing. Bricks were fired in kilns similar to this until fairly recent times at the Hudson River brick factories around Kingston, New York. In the nineteenth century, brickmakers in the Midwest traveled from town to town making bricks for local demand and firing in temporary scove kilns.

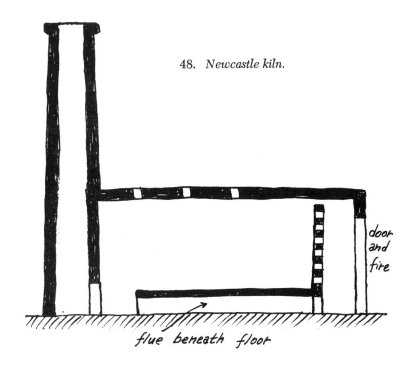

48. *Newcastle kiln.*

flue beneath floor

The Cassel kiln, popular in Germany for brick production, and its cousin, the Newcastle kiln in England, represent a break with the usual updraft systems. The Cassel kiln, Figure 47, consists of a rectangular chamber from 11 to 35 feet long and 8 to 12 feet high, with an arched roof. At the front of the kiln one or more fireplaces are provided. At the opposite end of the kiln is the doorway and above this is the chimney. Two or three feet from the front of the kiln a flash wall is erected which protects the setting from the direct impingement of flame and gives better heat distribution. In the bottom of the flash wall are three or more flues leading almost to the far end of the kiln and serving to convey some of the hot gases directly to the rear. The upper part of the flash wall is built of checker-work so as to admit the gases readily. The Cassel kiln is a crossdraft arrangement, and its advantage is a thorough transfer of heat to the ware and also the possibility of diverting or directing the hot gases, as desired, as they pass through the ware.

It will be seen that the Cassel kiln is similar in design to the Chinese kilns at Ching-tê-chên, and that no drastic changes are needed to make it into a downdraft kiln.

The Newcastle kiln is an English version of the Cassel kiln. It has its doorway through the fireplace, and the flash wall is rebuilt with each firing. Subfloor flues carry some of the flame directly towards the back of the kiln, helping to even out the distribution of heat. The entrance to the chimney is through a flue at the bottom of the back wall. This arrangement gives a partial downdraft effect.

The descendants of the Newcastle kiln in this country were the "ground hog" kilns used by the country potters of our southern highlands. These kilns, usually no more than eight or twelve feet long, were partially buried in earth to buttress the arch. A short chimney protruded from the mound of earth at the back.

For brick production, Newcastle kilns were constructed of great length, and to raise the temperature throughout, fuel was fed into the kiln through holes in the crown. The coal burned amid the setting which in the case of brick is no great hazard, especially if variations in color are not thought to be objectionable. It will be seen that Newcastle kilns of this kind are not different in principle from the old Korean kilns, except for the upward slope of the latter, certainly a good feature, since it increased the draft.

It should be noted that the improved design of kilns in Europe during the nineteenth century had to do entirely with the construction and draft of the kilns rather than with the fuel, for coal and wood continued to be the only fuels available for ceramic firing until oil began to be used in the early part of this century. Gas came even later, and electricity was not used for firing ceramics until after World War I.

Horizontal kilns of the Newcastle type are simple in design and easily constructed. The low, horizontal shape facilitates setting some types of ware. They are economical of fuel. However, temperatures are apt to vary from front to back, and the position of the fireplace may cause severe discoloration of wares placed toward the front of the kiln, since the heat is released from one point only.

The downdraft kiln avoids most of the disadvantages of other systems and may be considered the ultimate development in fuel burning kilns. The European downdraft kiln was either round or rectangular in shape. Figure 50 is a drawing of an early German downdraft kiln. The fireplaces are arranged at the sides, and the flames are deflected upwards and are then drawn down through the setting to flue holes at the bottom of the kiln and to a collecting flue below which leads to the chimney. In this system, the long pathway of the flame insures maximum heat transfer to the ware and chimney temperatures are reduced. Furthermore, by varying the height and permeability of the bag walls, and by adjusting the flameways through the setting and the size and position of the openings into the collecting flue, the distribution of heat can be closely controlled.

Figure 51 shows a round downdraft kiln. In this case, the fireplaces are arranged

49. Ben Owens, Jugtown potter, with his "ground hog" kiln. Photo, courtesy North Carolina State Department of Archives and History.

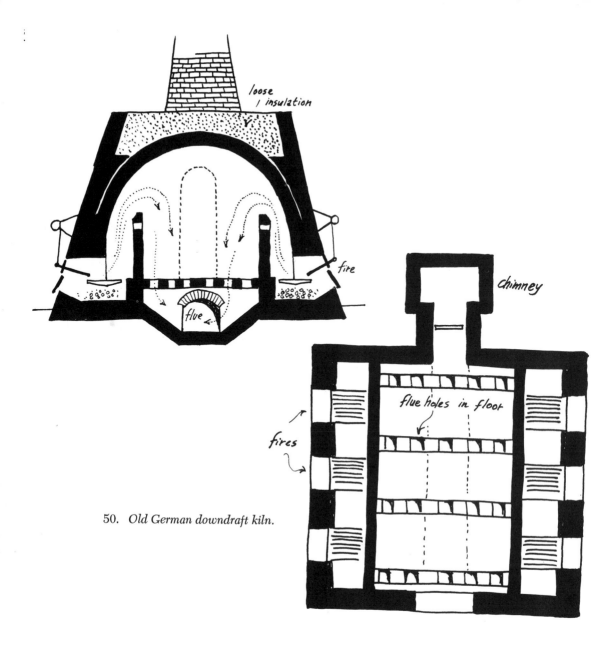

50. *Old German downdraft kiln.*

equidistantly around the perimeter of the kiln, and each fireplace has its own separate bag wall. Flue holes in the floor lead to a central collecting flue at the center, from which a flue passage leads underground to the chimney. Many designs have been made for flues in kilns of this type. Generally, many small openings in the floor are used. These may be partially closed off in spots that are too hot, forcing more of the hot gases toward other openings. In very large round kilns, rather elaborate connecting flues may be constructed under the floor. The principle is always the same: to draw the heat evenly down through the setting, and then to gather it up for exhaust through the chimney.

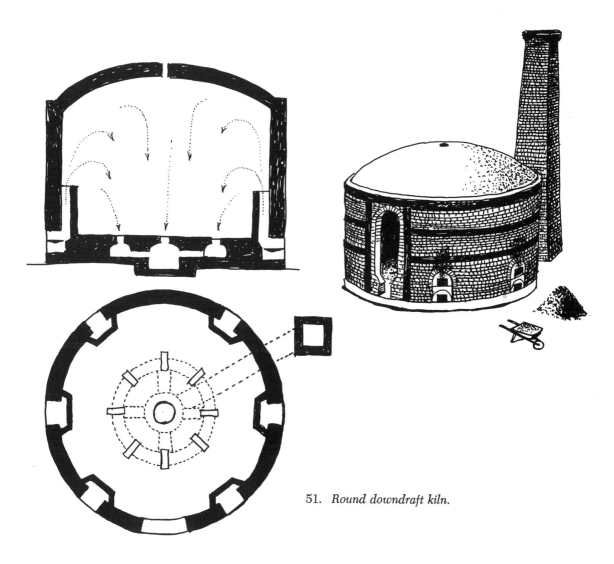

51. *Round downdraft kiln.*

It will be seen that since the downdraft kiln forces the heat downward, instead of allowing it to rise as it naturally tends to do, a strong pull is required through the chimney. This is especially true if the horizontal runs through the collecting flues are long or if the chimney must be at a distance from the kiln. The downdraft kiln, then, will require a larger and taller chimney than will an updraft or crossdraft kiln.

Besides the rectangular and round types noted above, there are many variations in the design of downdraft kilns. One variation is the use of several chimneys in the walls instead of having one main chimney into which all the flues lead. Chimneys built into the walls have the advantage of transfering some of the chimney heat back into the ware chamber, as shown in Figure 52, thus effecting a still further economy in fuel. This advantage, however, may be more than offset by the expense of building several chimneys, although each may be considerably shorter than that required by a single chimney kiln. Another variation leads part of the flame from the fireboxes to an opening in the center of the kiln, thus distributing the heat more evenly, as shown in Figure 53. This is perhaps useful only in the case of very large kilns. Another variation is the erection of a flue column in the center of the kiln, as shown in Figure 54. Here the hot gases enter holes near the bottom of the flue, which in effect is an interior chimney. Since this interior chimney

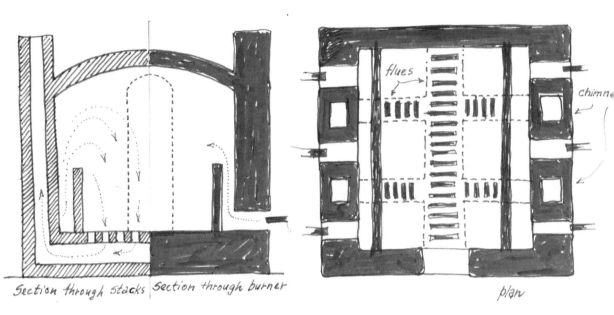

Section through stacks | Section through burner   plan

52. *Downdraft kiln with flues in the walls.*

is at the same temperature as the interior of the kiln but opens to the atmosphere above, it exerts a strong pull similar to that of the interior of an updraft kiln.

Double draft kilns, combining both the up and the downdraft systems, have been used especially for heavy products that require slow preliminary firing. In these kilns, a flue hole at the top of the dome is left open during the first part of the firing. When the ware is hot and sufficiently dried out, the hole is closed and the downdraft is begun through the bottom flues.

With the complete development of the downdraft kiln, the only other step needed to put western kilns at an equal level with those developed over a millennium earlier in China was the idea of connecting several chambers, thus conserving fuel by utilizing the waste heat from one chamber to warm the next. We have already seen how the bottle kiln did this by using what was in effect the lower part of the chimney for bisque firing. A great improvement on this idea was the two-stage kiln, in which the bottom was fired downdraft and the upper part was a simple updraft kiln for bisque. "Minton's Oven," patented in England in 1873, represents the ultimate refinement of this idea. As shown in Figure 55, the lower chamber

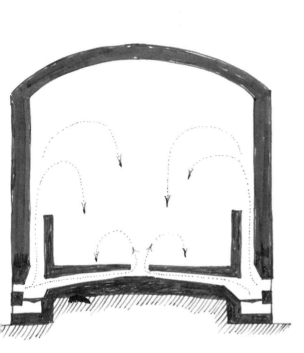

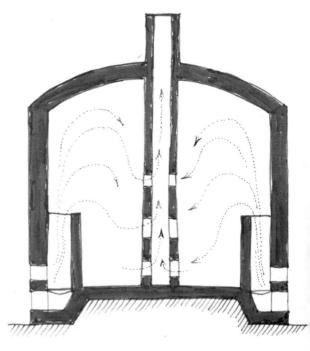

53. *Downdraft kiln with flues leading from the fires to the center of the kiln.*

54. *Downdraft kiln with interior flue.*

is a circular downdraft kiln. In this kiln the collecting flues in the floor lead to flues in the walls which lead upwards to the upper chamber. The fireplaces are at the sides as usual and have individual bag walls. An opening in the top of the lower chamber can be dampered off with a refractory plate, but when this hole is open the lower chamber works as an updraft, which is useful in the early stages of firing. The draft through the upper chamber is strong, requiring only a short chimney. A passage leading directly into the bottom of the kiln from the outside introduces cold air for cooling. It will be seen that Minton's kiln made maximum utilization of the heat from the fires. The ascending gases passing through the wall flues gave heat back into the lower chamber by radiation, an arrangement which prevented the temperature in the upper chamber from rising too high for bisque.

At the old Royal Copenhagen factory, a three-stage downdraft kiln was used

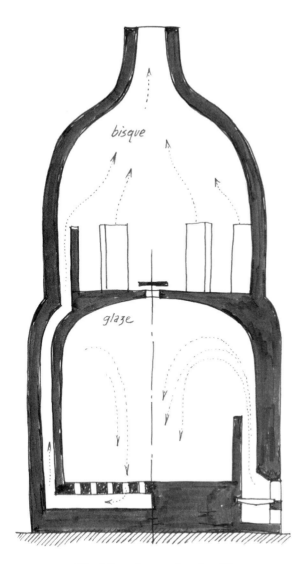

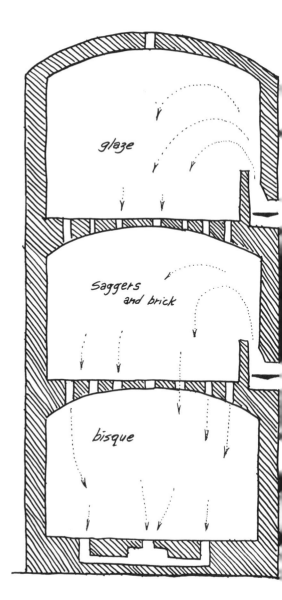

55. *Minton's two-chamber kiln.*

56. *Copenhagen three-chamber kiln.*

(Fig. 56). The two upper chambers have fireplaces and are vented through the bottom, one into the other. The lower chamber has no fireboxes, but collects the heat from the two upper chambers. The upper chamber was used for glost, the middle one for saggers and bricks, and the lower chamber for bisque. From our point of view these multiple-chambered kilns may seem primitive because they burned coal, but in their arrangements for heat circulation they are actually very sophisticated.

Many systems have been used to connect separate kiln chambers built at the same level, so that the exhaust heat from one would heat the next. These schemes, used largely in brick factories, take the heat from the flues of one downdraft chamber and pass it through a horizontal passageway into the air intake for the fireboxes of the next kiln. The difficulty is the long horizontal travel of the draft from one kiln to the next. Hence, connected kilns in Europe and America never reached the efficiency of the Oriental kilns, whose virtue lay in the upward slope of the series of chambers. Connected kilns have not been used for pottery or porcelain, except for the vertically stacked kilns described above.

A type of continuous kiln has been designed for bricks, however, which is very efficient because it makes complete use of the regenerative principle. As shown in Figure 57, the kiln is built like a ring made up of several chambers. These may be

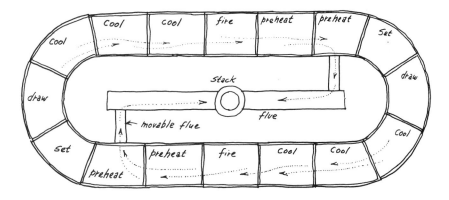

57. *Continuous kiln for firing brick.*

connected to the central chimney by the use of a movable flue. Each chamber is fired by introducing fuel among the bricks through holes at the top. Air for combustion is drawn from the neighboring chamber that is cooling, and exhaust heat is evacuated through the chamber on the other side that is being warmed up. Thus, the only heat wasted is that which seeps through the walls of the kiln. Continuous kilns of this type are obviously suited only for very large production. At any given time, one chamber is being fired, one being emptied, and the rest are either heating up or cooling down. The original continuous kiln was devised by Hoffmann and Licht in 1858 and was based on a study of the regenerative furnaces then used in metallurgy.

In industry, the most efficient kiln for large production is the tunnel kiln. In this type of kiln the ware is carried slowly on cars through a tunnel toward a hot zone in the middle during the heating cycle and then drawn out at the cooling end. It is not generally realized how early the first tunnel kilns were built. Apparently the first one was constructed at Vincennes, France, in 1751, and was used for firing overglaze decoration on porcelain. In 1840, Yordt patented a tunnel kiln in Denmark, and in England one was patented by E. Peters in 1858. While the principle of these early tunnel kilns was the same as those of today, it should be noted that they were not successful, mainly because of inadequate seals between the firing chambers and the mechanism of the cars. The first successful tunnel kiln was designed by O. Bock in England and patented in 1877. Bock's kiln had a sand seal similar to that employed today, but it had the disadvantage of being insufficiently long to give a good firing to the ware. Another difficulty with the early

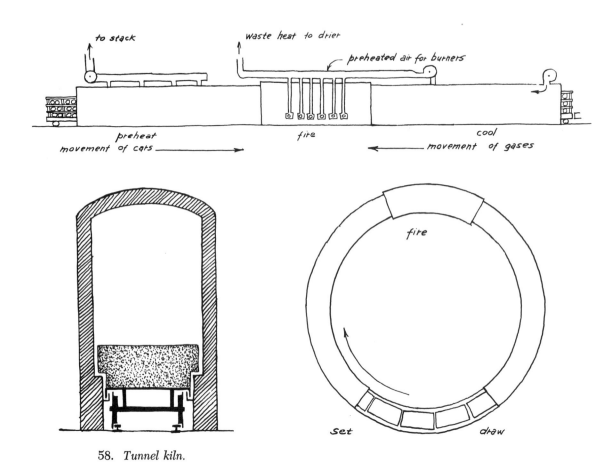

58. *Tunnel kiln.*

attempts to build tunnel kilns was the combustion of fuel, since oil and gas burners had not yet made their appearance. Bock's kiln was fired by dropping coal through openings in the crown of the kiln, which then burned among the setting of bricks. It is probable that no attempts were made to fire pottery in the early tunnel kilns, because the controls were not sufficiently exact for the relatively precise heat adjustments needed for glazes.

Many variations of the tunnel kiln were tried, but success had to wait for the development of efficient oil and gas burners. One intriguing early design, patented in England in 1908 by J. Boult, was a tunnel kiln incorporating a tank of water below it, on which barges floated the ware through the kiln.

Figure 58 shows a modern tunnel kiln in schematic essentials. As shown in the cross section, the metal wheels and top of the cars are sealed away from the heat by a sand seal. The cars are advanced slowly through the tunnel with a hydraulic pusher or other motor driven mechanism. Above, a system of ducts controls the distribution of heat. Hot air is taken from the cooling end by a blower, and supplied to the burners. Excess hot air is pumped to other parts of the shop for drying or heating. An exhaust fan at the entrance of the kiln draws warm air into the preheating section. Thus most of the heat is utilized. The great advantage of the tunnel kiln is that no heat is wasted in the periodic heating and cooling of the kiln itself. Constant heat also lengthens the life of the kiln, since it is not subjected to the alternating expansion and contraction caused by heating and cooling. The firing cycle can be readily adjusted by controlling the speed of the cars. A further great advantage of the tunnel kiln is that the setting and drawing of the cars may be done in the open.

Obviously, a large and steady production is needed to justify a tunnel kiln, while small scale or intermittent production is still best fired in periodic kilns.

Straight tunnel kilns are built with a spare track beside them on which the cars are returned to the entrance, where they are reset with ware. Some tunnels kilns are built on a circular plan, as shown in Figure 58. Although the construction of such kilns is more complex, there is an advantage in having the unloading and loading at the same station, especially in the case of a small kiln operated by one man.

The art of building periodic kilns was quite complete by the year 1900, with the exception of two aspects of the kiln which were more fully developed in the twentieth century. These were, first, the introduction of oil and gas for fuel and the perfection of fuel burners, and, second, the development of improved refractories, especially insulating refractories. It is interesting to note that A. B. Searle in his book *Kilns and Kiln Building*, published in 1915,[1] makes no mention of insulation or insulating refractories. At that time there were no oil-fired kilns in England, and the only gas kilns were those few that used producer or coal gas.

Pyrometry, or the measurement and control of temperature, has also reached a high stage of development since its beginnings around 1900.

---

[1] Searle, A. B. *Kilns and Kiln Building* (London: The Clayworker Press, 1915).

PART 2

The Design and Construction of Kilns

1

Fuels, Burners, and Combustion

ALL KILNS OPERATE through the release of heat-energy. This release must be achieved by the combustion of fuel. Electric kilns, an exception to this, are discussed separately. They utilize the radiant heat created by electrical resistance.

A distinction should be made between heat and temperature. Heat refers to the quantity of heat-energy released and is measured in B.t.u.'s or calories. The B.t.u. or British thermal unit is the amount of heat required to raise one pint of water one degree Fahrenheit. A calorie is the amount of heat required to raise one cubic centimeter of water one degree Centigrade. Temperature, or the intensity of heat, is measured in degrees Centigrade or degrees Fahrenheit. One degree Centigrade is 1/100 of the temperature differential between boiling and freezing water.

Combustion involves the reaction of a carbonaceous fuel with oxygen and the attendant release of heat. The reaction of combustion may be expressed in the chemical formula: $C + O_2 \overset{\text{HEAT}}{=} CO_2$. Thus the carbon is converted to the gas carbon dioxide.

The carbon cycle of nature is an interesting phenomenon. It is believed that in remote geological ages, before the advent of life, there was more carbon dioxide in the air than at present. Plants learned to fixate this carbon in their structures. This is accomplished by photosynthesis, a process in which the plant, through the action of sunlight on its leaves, forms complex hydrocarbons from water, air, and carbon dioxide. The residues of dead plants are almost pure carbon and survive on earth in vast quantities in the fossil forms of coal and oil. Animals utilize oxygen from the air to oxidize plants as food, exhaling carbon dioxide as a waste product, making it again available to plants. The burning of any carbonaceous materials such as wood, coal, oil or grass likewise releases carbon dioxide into the air.

Combustion of carbonaceous matter occurs in the presence of oxygen whenever the kindling temperature is reached, and as we know from practical experience, fire is sustained as long as fuel and air are available. In practice, arrangements for combustion vary with the nature of the fuel, whether it be solid, liquid, or gaseous. In each case, the problem is to bring the fuel into contact with enough oxygen-bearing air to support complete combustion. All solid and liquid fuels must be converted to gas before combustion begins. Conversion of a solid fuel to a gas is brought about through an increase in temperature, and the higher the temperature, the greater the conversion speed.

Solid fuels are difficult to burn, because oxygen can only reach the surface and the mass burns only as it is eaten away or consumed by fire. Solid fuels burn more readily when reduced to smaller unit size.

Wood, coal, or coke is best burned on a grate to hold the fuel up so air can circulate under, around, and through the burning mass. Anyone who tends a fireplace has learned that the secret of a lively blaze is getting the air to the fire. Grates are made of bars of iron or clay that will withstand the heat. As the firing proceeds, ash residues drop through the grate to an ash pit below, as shown in Figure 43. Unless provision is made for the ash to drop away from the fire, its accumulation will choke off air for combustion and slow down the fire. To insure a continuous influx of air, a draft is necessary; a strong and steady pull must be established in the kiln and chimney to draw in air at the point of combustion. The need for a positive inrush of air in solid fuel burning kilns usually requires a fairly high chimney.[1] Adjustable openings to admit air below the grate bar level provide control for oxidation and reduction. An excess of draft capacity is desirable for flexibility of operation.

Some wood burning grates for kilns are operated on an upsidedown system, as shown in Figure 59. In this system, the wood is piled on the grate and the bottom pieces burn first. Ash residues drop through the grate, allowing the pieces above to drop down toward the grate where they ignite and burn. The advantage of this arrangement is that a stack of wood can be left on the grate and the fire will feed itself unattended until the whole stack is burned. Such an arrangement requires a strong draft and has the disadvantage of not working well until the firing has reached a certain intensity.

Ample space must be allowed for the combustion of solid fuels, and even in small kilns the grate must be large enough to take sufficient fuel to liberate the necessary quantities of heat. For this reason, very small wood- or coal-burning kilns are impractical, because too high a percentage of the total space must be given over to combustion.

[1] Oriental chamber kilns, which have no chimneys, nevertheless develop a strong draft because the entire kiln is built on an upward slope.

Burning solid fuel usually involves intermittent stoking, and there must be ample flue area to take care of sudden bursts of hot gases. Often a blow hole is opened in the crown of the kiln during stoking to permit the easy escape of smoke and flame. In general, solid fuel burning kilns need large flues and high, generous chimneys.

Soft woods with an open grain structure are preferred for kiln firing. It might be thought that the hardwoods, which have a higher potential in total heat released per pound of wood, would be more preferable. However, the soft woods actually

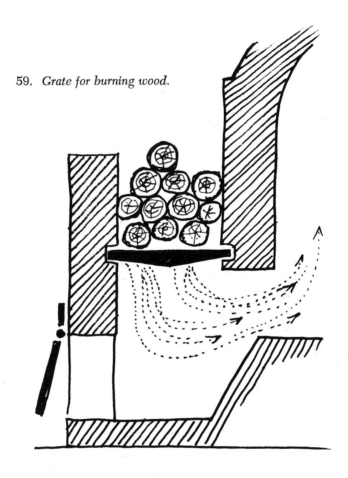

59. *Grate for burning wood.*

yield more heat because the heat is released at a faster rate, an important factor in raising the temperature of a kiln. Woods such as pine, fir, hemlock, or spruce make excellent fuel, and if a source of supply of such woods is available, the firing cost may be comparable to the cost of firing with oil or gas, or even less. But constant attendance at the firing and the necessary labor of splitting, storing, and drying the wood weigh against wood as a practical fuel.

60. *Wood burning catenary arch kiln built by John Jessiman at Cortland, N. Y.*

61. *Two-chamber wood burning kiln built by William Alexander at Ft. Collins, Colo. The domes were made of cone-shaped brick made especially for this kiln.*

Coal has been widely used in Europe as a fuel for kilns, as it releases a great deal of heat for its weight and bulk. However, the sulphurous gases released by burning coal make the use of saggers necessary, and the high ember temperature of coal causes grates to deteriorate rapidly. Sawdust, which is sometimes used for space heating in the Northwest, might be a good fuel for kilns if a proper burner could be devised.

Grass, brush, reeds, leaves, or any other dry organic matter can be used; but the difficulty of gathering, storing, drying, and stoking these lighter fuels seems to rule them out on practical grounds.

There has been renewed interest in wood as a fuel for pottery firing because of the possible textures which may result from flashing and from the deposit of ash on the ware. Aside from these benefits, the management of wood burning kilns offers a sense of participation in the firing process which is entirely lacking in electric firing and which may be minimal in the case of oil or gas. Simple wood-fired kilns may be ideal for camp projects or for the amateur who wishes to return to basic processes, especially if there is a source of inexpensive wood at hand.

Contrary to popular opinion, the use of wood or coal instead of gas or oil does not mean any serious limitation of temperature, and with a well-designed kiln,

62. *Temporary wood burning kiln built by students at the Haystack School, Deer Isle, Maine. Photo by Michael Cohen.*

63. *Kiln at Abuja, Northern Nigeria. This kiln was designed and built under the supervision of Michael Cardew, and is similar to one he built for his own pottery in England. Photo by Francis Uher, courtesy, Nigerian Minister of Information.*

64. *Back of the Abuja kiln. Photo by Francis Uher.*

65. *Potter at Abuja. Photo by Francis Uher.*

temperatures in excess of 1300° C. can be reached. At that heat, the roar of combustion and the white hot intensity of the fireboxes let one know that a firing is really in process, and each new piece of wood tossed into the inferno almost explodes into pure incandescent heat. It is exciting.

Management of a wood fire requires some experience and considerable care. The wood must be split down to pieces of the proper size and must be thoroughly dry. If the wood is even slightly damp, the heat required to volatilize the water as steam will tend to cancel any gain in temperature. It is wise to provide a drying rack near or over the kiln where the fuel can be stored until used. In Japan the potters pile

66. *Placing saggers inside the Abuja kiln. Photo by Francis Uher.*

their bundles of wood directly on the top of the kiln to insure dryness. Wood must be fed in at the proper rate; if not enough is added, the temperature in the kiln may drop precipitously, especially if the damper is open and cold air is being pulled in through the grate. But if too much wood is piled on, the fire may be temporarily smothered, causing a loss rather than a gain in heat. Steady stoking of a few pieces of wood at intervals of about 5 minutes usually gives the best rate of climb. It is seldom necessary to remove ashes from the ash pit during the firing, but it may be necessary to rake them smooth to insure the entry of plenty of air from below the grate. An iron tool similar to a hoe is useful for this.

Firing with wood inevitably produces a great deal of smoke, and for this reason the location of the kiln should be carefully considered. A well ventilated kiln shed, standing by itself and with its separate chimney, is the ideal situation. Lacking a reasonably isolated site, one must have tolerant neighbors.

The ash that is drawn through the kiln in wood firing affects the pyrometric cones. Wood ash contains many alkalies and these fuse with the cone, causing it to melt at a temperature somewhat lower than normal. This difficulty can be avoided by making a little clay "house" or roof over the cone plaque, to shield it from the deposit of ashes. In stoneware, the influence of the deposited ash on the glazes is often esthetically welcome. Accidental mottling of color and texture may be noted on the shoulders of jars and on the horizontal surfaces of plates or lids. If the clay contains even a small amount of iron, flashings of brown to reddish brown will be noted where the flames have licked about the pots. The wood fire produces a long flame, extending through the entire setting to the flues.

It is possible to obtain a clear or oxidizing fire with wood, but if the most efficient rate of climb is maintained the atmosphere tends to be neutral or slightly reducing. This accounts for the fact that almost all pottery in China and Japan was fired in reduction or partial reduction; that was the most efficient and economical way of reaching the desired temperature.

Firing with oil presents some difficulties and requires rather more equipment than other fuels, but since oil is fairly cheap and available everywhere it may be the most practical fuel.

67. *B.t.u. ratings of various fuels.*

Natural gas	950—1050 B.t.u./cu. ft.
Butane gas	3210 B.t.u./cu. ft.
Propane gas	2558 B.t.u./cu. ft., or 93,500 B.t.u./gallon
#2 Fuel oil	135,000—139,000 B.t.u./gallon
Electricity	29.3 K.W.H./100,000 B.t.u.
Air dried hickory wood	24,200,000 B.t.u./cord
Air dried aspen wood	12,300,000 B.t.u./cord

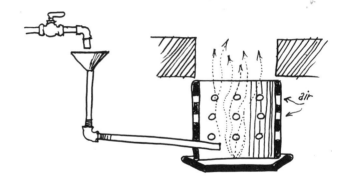

68. *Drip oil burner.*

The problem in burning oil is to break up the liquid into vapor, small droplets or mist, and to bring air to the oil so it may ignite and burn. Since oil is widely used as a commercial fuel, a great deal of engineering talent has been devoted to the design of oil burners. There are innumerable types of oil burners on the market, most of them rather too complex and efficient for pottery kilns. The simplest oil burners, though certainly not the most efficient, are based on the idea of volatilizing oil on a hot surface. An updraft burner of the "drip" type is illustrated in Figure 68. The oil feeds by gravity to a valve from which it is dripped into a funnel and pipe leading to a cast iron pan. Here it is ignited, and the flame is drawn up through a cast iron collar, with perforations in it to admit air. The air mixes with the volatilized oil, and combustion occurs as the flame enters the kiln. Radiant heat from the kiln heats the iron plate so that when the oil drips onto it, it rises instantly as a vapor and is ignited.

This type of burner works very well when hot, but may burn with considerable smoke in the early stages of firing. Incomplete combustion of oil sometimes causes the growth of a carbon clinker above the burner. This may have to be broken up with a poker.

Another type of drip oil burner which operates horizontally and is therefore better adapted to downdraft kilns, is shown in Figure 69. A steel tube about 6 inches square and 12 inches long is set into the wall of the kiln. Welded into the tube are two plates set at angles as shown. Oil enters the tube in a small pipe, dripping onto the first plate, where it ignites. Any oil not burned on the first plate drips off onto the second, burning there. When the burner is hot, most of the oil is completely volatilized in the burner and mixed with the air drawn into the end of the tube. A sliding plate controls the amount of air. As in the case of the first drip burners described, this device works well when hot, but will give a rather smokey flame during the early stages of the firing. Some device for mixing a small amount of water with the oil will improve combustion in the drip burner. Although such burners have given satisfactory service over many firings, prolonged usage will oxidize the steel tube, making the life of the burner relatively short.

The advantage of drip-style burners is that there are no moving parts to go out of order. The oil is fed by gravity, so no pump is needed. The oil tanks need be

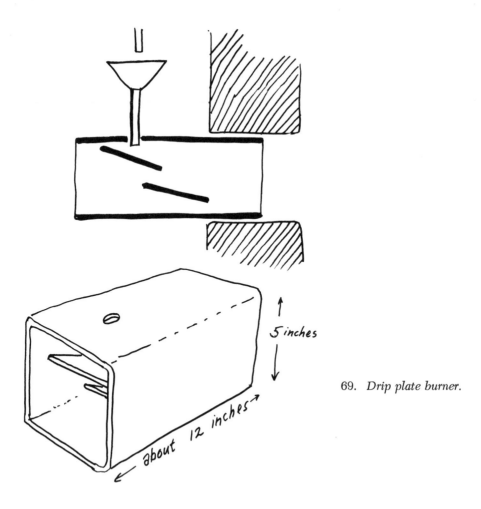

69. *Drip plate burner.*

elevated only a few feet above the burner to give an adequate flow. For safety, a fairly long run of pipe is recommended, so the oil tank will be at least 15 feet away from the kiln, and preferably outside the building. A 200-gallon oil tank of the type used for household space heating is adequate for small kilns. A strainer should be provided at the exit of the tank to prevent clogging. A reasonably well insulated kiln of 20 cubic foot capacity may take about 50 to 75 gallons of oil to fire. It is wise to have an ample reserve capacity in the tank.

For drip burners, kerosene or number 2 diesel fuel may be used. Kerosene volatilizes easily but does not yield quite as many B.t.u.'s per gallon as the heavier diesel fuel. Oils heavier than number 2 diesel will not burn efficiently in drip burners.

More efficient and more mechanically complex types of oil burners involve the use of air under pressure or both air and oil under pressure. A low pressure burner of the "Denver" type has proved to be very satisfactory for ceramic kilns. As shown in Figure 72, the oil is fed by gravity to an adjustable needle valve, escaping through a small orifice at A. Air fed from a blower enters at B and can be adjusted with a butterfly valve. The air mixes with the oil as it exists at C, breaking it up into

70. *Door of Bernard Leach's kiln at St. Ives, England. Photo by Michael Cohen.*

71. *Oil burner of Leach's kiln. Photo by Michael Cohen.*

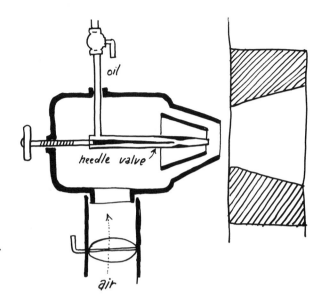

72. *Denver type oil burner.*

a mist composed of small droplets. As secondary air is pulled into the burner port, which may have a conical shape, complete combustion occurs. By adjusting the flow of both air and oil, the intensity and mixture of the blaze can be closely controlled. A burner of this type requires a blower, which may feed two or more burners if a suitable manifold is provided. To operate two burners, a blower with a casing of about 16 inches in diameter, running at 3500 rpm and generating at least four ounces of pressure will be required.

73. *Drip feed warmup for oil-fired kiln.*

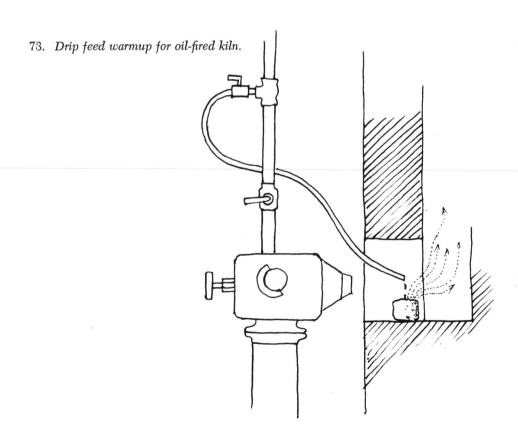

In the early stages of firing, a drip feed to the burner ports may be contrived, as shown in Figure 74. Oil is fed through a flexible copper tube onto a small piece of insulating brick. With this arrangement, the advance of heat can be closely controlled, and when the main burners are turned on, they work well because the burner port is already hot.

A homemade oil burner may be constructed from pipe fittings, as shown in Figure 74. This burner works fairly well, especially if the oil tank is elevated to about eight feet or more above the burner, giving sufficient head to the oil pressure to cause a lively squirt from the small orifice. The nozzle may be shaped by cutting the small end off a $1\frac{1}{2}$ to 1 inch bell-reducer fitting. As with other low-pressure oil burners, the operation is fairly efficient when the burner port is red hot,

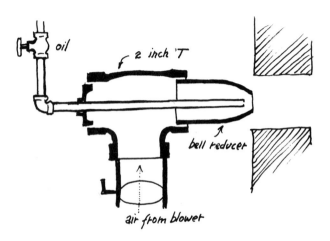

74. *Oil burner made from pipe fittings.*

but not so successful in the early stages of the fire. The position of the orifice in the air nozzle is critical for the best breakup of the oil. It should be just back of the end of the nozzle. The burner should be placed so the nozzle is slightly inside the port, where it will be warmed by the fire. Discarded vacuum cleaner blowers have been used for improvised oil burners.

Since oil burners of the type described depend on a motor driven blower to supply the air, a power failure can be dangerous. Without an air supply the burning oil may run down the outside of the kiln. Careful supervision of the firing is absolutely necessary. A valuable safety feature on any oil-fired kiln is a solenoid valve which will shut off the oil supply in case the electricity fails.

In the more efficient types of oil burners, oil is pumped under pressure and ejected through a very small orifice. Higher air pressure or steam pressure is used to volatilize the oil more completely. When an oil pump is used, the oil can be forced through a very small orifice, which helps to break it up into a mist, and high pressure air, released through a narrow opening, will pulverize the mist into a vapor, putting it into an ideal form for combustion. In some burners a centrifugal device is used for ejecting the oil into a mixing chamber. These more sophisticated oil burners are used for industrial and household heating, where the temperature of the furnace remains relatively low, thus necessitating rapid and efficient combustion. For kiln firing, however, where the firebox is at red heat or more, simpler burners are equally effective. Simpler burners are preferable for kilns because there is less that can go wrong with them. Highly efficient oil burners with complete safety controls are expensive, often costing as much as the kiln itself or even more.

The kerosene torch has sometimes been used to fire kilns. This is designed for space heating, melting roofing tar, and for weed burning. The fuel is supplied from a tank kept under pressure with a hand pump and ejected from a small orifice into a heated mixing nozzle. A long powerful flame can be produced, with ample release of heat to fire a small kiln. Torch burners are usually given a temporary mounting outside the burner port. The tendency of the kerosene torch to become clogged is a serious disadvantage.

Oil fuel produces good results in ceramic kilns. The atmosphere can be easily controlled. A very rapid advance of heat is possible if desired, and the cost of fuel is not excessive. But there are serious drawbacks. Oil storage is space consuming, and there is always some smell and dirt. The noise of the blower is a disadvantage in most situations. The oil flame has a damaging effect on the refractories of the kiln, and in time causes slagging and cracking. The danger of fire must also be considered. No matter how carefully managed, oil firing is a potential danger. Another disadvantage of oil is the necessity for constant watching and adjustment during the firing. And in some cases, the smoke which develops from the chimney in the early stages of firing may be very objectionable, to the neighbors if not to the potter.

These considerations have led most ceramists to choose liquified petroleum gas as a fuel rather than oil, even though the cost per firing is usually considerably more. In most respects, gas is the ideal fuel for kilns. It is safe, easily burned, cheap, and gives perfect results. Unlike oil burners, gas burners are simple, inexpensive and foolproof.

Natural gas is much to be preferred to coal gas or producer gas. The latter are manufactured from coal and have less B.t.u.'s per cubic foot than natural gas. Moreover, coal gas contains sulphur, which may be damaging to glazes. Where only producer gas is available, it may be better to choose liquified petroleum gas as a fuel.

The simplest gas burner is the atmospheric burner or inspirating burner. As shown in Figure 75, it consists of a cast iron tube A into which the gas is introduced through a small orifice B. The flow of gas is controlled by a valve C. When the gas enters the tube, it entrains air through the openings D, and the gas and air are mixed as they move through the tube, burning at the exit. The tube is shaped with a constriction just beyond the point where the gas exits, and this feature is called the venturi.[1] The constriction causes an increase of speed in the flow of gas, and a

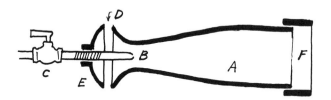

75. *Atmospheric or inspirating gas burner.*

76. *Burner for liquified propane. The liquid fuel is ejected from a small orifice under pressure. The surrounding collar becomes heated and heats the fuel to the vaporizing point as it approaches the orifice through the coil.*

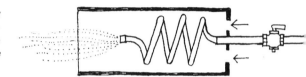

slight vacuum is created, drawing air into the burner. The amount of air is controlled by adjusting the position of the round plate E. The end of the tube may be fitted with a heat-resistant cast iron tip F. Adjustment of air and gas will give the desired oxidizing, neutral or reducing flame. Burners of this type work well even at low adjustment, and the only thing that can go wrong is the propagation of the flame back into the tube. This "coughing" is caused by an excess of air and can be prevented by decreasing the air supply at E.

A version of the atmospheric gas burner can be made from pipe fittings, as shown in Figure 77. A is a 1½-inch pipe, into which a ½-inch pipe is fitted with reducing fittings at B. A pipe cap with a 1/32-inch hole drilled in it serves as an orifice at C, gas is controlled through valve D, and air is controlled through holes at E, fitted with a perforated slipping collar, which can widen or narrow the holes in the tube depending on its position. This burner lacks the venturi shape and does not entrain air as efficiently as a factory made burner, but it works quite satisfactorily, nevertheless. The orifice should be positioned just ahead of the air holes.

[1] The venturi principle was discovered in 1797 by the Italian scientist Venturi.

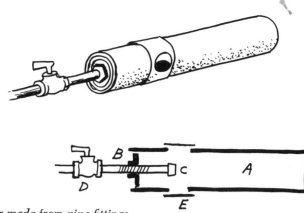

77. *Atmospheric gas burner made from pipe fittings.*

Another homemade burner, shown in Figure 78, has come to be called the "Alfred" burner. It uses 2-inch pipe fittings and is suitable for larger kilns. A 2-inch cross fitting is attached below to a ½-inch gas pipe entering through reducers. This pipe is fitted with a drilled pipe cap, which forms the orifice, and with a valve below. One side of the fitting is provided with a metal flap which can be adjusted for air. The other side is provided with a 2-inch plug. The gas-air mixture travels up the pipe and into the burner port where it ignites. The plug can be removed

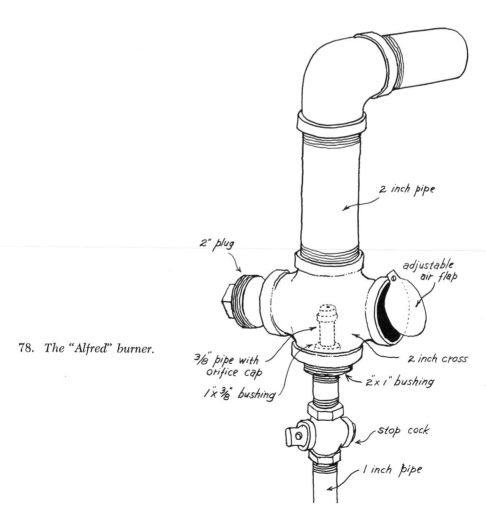

78. *The "Alfred" burner.*

by hand, enabling the operator to screw on orifice caps of various sizes, thus controlling the flow of gas. By using several sized orifice caps, installed in the burner at various stages of the firing, a highly reproducible firing curve can be achieved that is not dependent on the operation of valves.

Operation of the atmospheric burners described above requires gas pressure of at least 6 ounces. If available, gas pressure of between 1 and 2 pounds is an advantage. The pressure of gas furnished for household use is usually 6 to 8 ounces, ample for good combustion provided a sufficient volume of gas is available.

Before installing a gas kiln it is well to consider the gas supply carefully, and to consult with the supplying utility company. Since kilns burn an unusual amount of gas the meter at the site may be too small to pass sufficient gas, even though the pressure is adequate. Gas suppliers are usually agreeable to installing larger meters if that is necessary. Another difficulty often encountered is the distance between the meter and the kiln. If this distance is too great, a loss of volume and pressure will occur, and insufficient gas may reach the kiln. If the meter is set for 6 ounces of pressure and the kiln is 20 feet from the meter, a line of pipe at least 1 inch in diameter will be required. If the kiln is more than 20 feet away from the meter the line may have to be of 1½-inch pipe or even 2-inch pipe. Consultation with the gas company is advised to solve these problems before kiln construction begins.

Factors such as the size of the kiln, the temperatures required, and the pressure in the gas main all have a bearing on the problem, and it is difficult to prescribe the details of an installation until all these variables are known. For larger kilns, 20 cu. ft. or more, pressures higher than 8 ounces are desirable, and if the kiln can be connected as a commercial furnace, the utility company may provide more pressure. Local practice and zoning regulations, however, often rule out the possibility of increased pressure.

Another type of gas burner employs forced air. Forced-air burners give excellent gas-air mixture with good control of the ratio. Forced-air gas burners are seldom used on smaller ceramic kilns because the refinement of control which they offer is not really necessary, and because their greater cost and complexity is not justified by the job to be done. Figure 79 illustrates a forced-air gas burner. A is a motor driven fan. Air from it passes a butterfly valve B and enters a tube in which gas is introduced through valve C. The gas and air are mixed and ejected at the burner port where they ignite. A U-tube manometer may be provided at D which gives an accurate relative indication of the amount of gas flowing into the burner. As a burner of this type is dependent on electric current, power failure will result in a heavily reducing flame. Safety requires careful attendance during the firing, and a solenoid valve to shut off the gas in case the electricity fails is recommended. Forced air burners are rather touchy to operate and any slight change of setting of either the gas or the air may make considerable difference in kiln atmosphere and rate of temperature advance. The forced-air gas burner is capable of high output, and is useful where a very rapid heating cycle is desired. More air, and

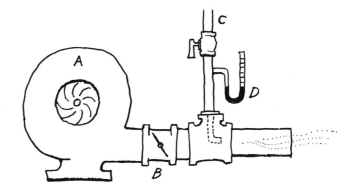

79. *Forced-air gas burner.*

therefore more gas, can be introduced, giving a powerful flame. Another advantage is that no secondary air entering around the burner port is needed, so it is unnecessary to have a strong draft in the kiln. This may be an important advantage where connection to a chimney is impractical. The kiln equipped with forced-air burners may be equipped with a hood through which the cooled exhaust gases may be vented through the roof or a window.

Another type of forced-air gas burner sometimes used for kilns premixes the gas and air in the blower itself. As shown in Figure 80, gas is led through a valve A and directly into the blower, where it is churned up with the air and ejected into the burner port. The air supply is controlled through a slot valve on the blower B. A burner of this type is highly efficient, and in some designs, the control of both gas and air is linked to one control lever, assuring the correct mixture at any given volume. This makes adjustment for reduction firing rather difficult, however. Premixed gas and air produces a short, hot flame, which tends to bring the firebox and the immediately surrounding area to a high temperature relative to the rest of the interior of the kiln. It is perhaps not the best type of gas burner for an even distribution of heat. Even heating of the kiln is favored by burners producing a large volume of hot gases, as is the case in atmospheric types, rather than by a smaller volume of higher temperature gases.

80. *Premix gas burner.*

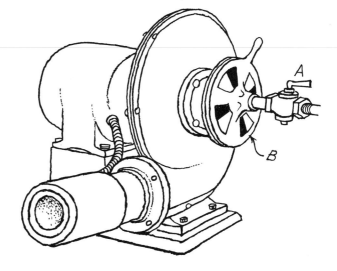

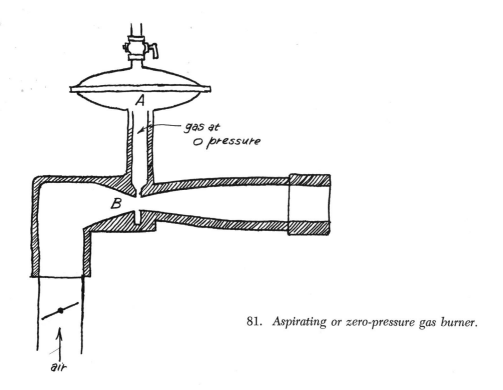

81. *Aspirating or zero-pressure gas burner.*

Zero-pressure gas burners, or aspirating burners, employ another principle, as shown in Figure 81. Gas is led into a diaphragm A, which reduces its pressure to atmospheric pressure. Air from a blower passes a venturi, B, where it entrains the gas, and the mixture is ejected into the burner port where it ignites. This type of burner operates on a principle opposite to that of the atmospheric burner; the gas is entrained by the air rather than vice versa. The volume of gas-air is controlled entirely by the volume of air which is fed to the burner. More air passing the venturi will pick up more gas. Setting the diaphragm for slightly more or less gas pressure will control the gas-air ratio of the mixture. The zero-pressure burner is seldom used on small pottery kilns, but is useful on commercial kilns where an exact advance of temperature can be controlled by intermittently activating the blower through feedback from a pyrometer.

Devices for burning natural gas are very simple in design and operation. Almost as simple and reliable are the systems used for burning liquified petroleum gas, known as LPG. LPG is actually a by-product of the petroleum industry, and is widely used as a fuel where natural gas is not available. Propane and butane are liquified petroleum gases with somewhat differing vapor pressures, which are sometimes sold under trade names. LPG is delivered to the customer in tanks, or is supplied in bulk to tanks owned by the consumer. Vaporization of the liquid in the tank creates a gas under pressure. When some of the gas is drawn off in use, more is formed as a result of the drop in pressure. The pressure in the line to the burners is controlled by a diaphragm regulator, and this pressure may be as high as one or two pounds per square inch, even from a small tank.

Burners for LPG may be similar to ones used for natural gas. Simple atmospheric burners work very well. Since the pressure of the gas is high, the orifice of the burner must be small, usually smaller than that used for natural gas. In operation, there must be ample tank capacity for the intended rate of use, for if too much gas is evaporated from a given sized tank, the LPG may freeze due to the temperature drop which attends evaporation. For firing an average sized kiln it is necessary to secure a large tank of 500 gallon capacity or more, or to hook four or five 100 lb. tanks in tandem with a manifold which draws from all tanks equally. Suppliers of LPG will sell or rent tanks of suitable size and they will advise as to the proper size of tank and the equipment necessary for connection to the burners. Suppliers will know best how to comply with local safety regulations.

A disadvantage of LPG as a fuel is the need to provide storage tanks and to keep them full, and the relatively higher cost. As to the latter, LPG firing seldom exceeds twice the cost of natural gas, and this extra cost is usually not a deciding factor, especially if oil, with its various drawbacks, is the alternative. The operation of a kiln burning LPG is similar to one burning natural gas and the only added consideration is the provision of an ample reserve to see the firing through.

LPG does have one bad feature; it is heavier than air, and if a leak occurs, the gas collects along the floor or finds its way into a basement where it can ignite and cause an explosion. Great care must be taken to insure that there are no leaks in valves or fittings leading up to the kiln.

It is difficult to estimate the quantity of fuel which any kiln will require because of the variables involved. A well constructed wood-fired kiln of about 30 cu. ft. capacity can be fired to cone 8 with about two cords of wood. More will be required if the wood is damp or improperly split.

An oil burner like the one illustrated in Figure 72 will burn a maximum of about 5 gallons of fuel oil per hour. This rate of consumption would occur only at the height of firing; much less would be consumed during most of the firing. A 30 cu. ft. gas kiln may burn about 1000 cu. ft. of natural gas per hour, and to fire to cone 9 may require 7000 or 8000 cubic feet.

These figures are approximations. Factors such as construction of the kiln, type of burners, height of chimney, atmosphere of firing, method of setting the ware, and rate of firing will all affect the consumption of fuel.

From the above summary of possible fuels for ceramic kilns the potter's choice should be clear. The romantic, or the potter operating in a remote place, may choose wood. Those who have natural gas will be wise to use it. Those who have no natural gas must choose between oil and LPG, and increasingly the choice is for the latter. Those who can afford two kilns may choose both gas and wood, for variety. Electric kilns, in some ways the most practical of all, but certainly not the most versatile or exciting, are discussed in a later section.

2

Refractory Materials

WE HAVE SEEN how heat may be generated and introduced into the kiln, and must now consider ways of retaining it there so it may do its work on the objects being fired. Surprisingly, there are very few materials, natural or otherwise, which are sufficiently heat resistant to be used for kilns reaching 1000° C. or more.

An examination of the melting points of the elements as shown on the periodic table will show seven main types of chemical substances with high refractoriness, or resistance to heat. These are the oxides, carbides, nitrides, silicides, sulphides, borides, and single elements. The melting points of some of these refractory substances are shown in the chart, Figure 82. The most refractory oxide, Thoria (ThO_2), has a melting point of just over 3000° C. Carbon is the most refractory element. The most refractory of all known substances are hafnium and tantalum carbides, which have melting points of around 4000° C. The usefulness of the carbides, nitrides, silicides, sulphides, borides, and most single elements, is severely limited by their tendency to oxidize at high temperature when exposed to air. For all practical purposes, this rules them out for industrial use unless they can be suitably protected or are used for very short time applications. (Silicon Carbide is somewhat of an exception to this; it is a useful refractory material because when it begins to oxidize at high temperature a glaze of silica is formed on its surface, giving it some protection from further oxidation.) Strictly speaking, only the refractory oxides can be used indefinitely at high temperatures when exposed to air. Twenty-four oxides have melting points of 1725° C. or over. One might think that with this large group of refractory oxides available there would be many choices for furnace building, but this is not the case. Several oxides have a very limited usefulness because they hydrate on cooling, dissociate to lower oxides at high temperatures, or are so scarce as to be prohibitively expensive.

Five pure oxides may be considered useful as refractories at very high temperatures (in excess of 1800° C.). They are Al_2O_3, MgO, BeO, ZrO_2, and ThO_2. These pure oxides are scarce, however, and refractories for commercial use are made mostly from naturally occurring rocks and minerals composed of them. When we consider those materials which are common enough to be processed commercially, yet are resistant enough to heat to serve as refractories, the list becomes very small indeed.

The most useful and the most available refractory material is clay. Pure kaolin or kaolinite ($Al_2O_3 \cdot 2SiO_2 \cdot 2H_2O$) has a melting point of 1785° C. Since almost all clays in commercial deposits contain impurities such as iron, and at least traces of alkalies and other oxides in addition to alumina and silica, the melting point of any available clay, no matter how pure, is below that figure. Even common red-burning surface clay is quite refractory and heat resistant compared to most materials. Once clay has been fired it becomes very stable and may be reheated again and again with little change occurring. An ordinary red brick, which is usually fired at the factory to about 1000° C., will withstand perhaps 1100° without melting, bloating or deforming. Some buff colored bricks used for building will withstand even higher temperatures. Early kilns were commonly built of red bricks, and these were entirely satisfactory for low-temperature firings.

For firings of 1000° C. or higher, more refractory bricks made of fireclay or kaolin must be used. Fireclay may be defined as any clay that will withstand the higher temperatures. Bricks made from fireclay are usually made with considerable grog and are fired at about cone 10 or higher. They are hard, dense, volume stable, resistant to cracking and spalling, and are easily cut and worked into masonry structures. Firebricks are such a basic necessity to so many industries involving heat treatment processes that they are manufactured in enormous quantities and may be purchased in any town.

Clays suitable for the manufacture of firebrick are quite common. Such clays are often found in connection with seams of coal, and may have a considerable quantity of iron impurities. They vary a great deal in plasticity. The clay is mined, ground, and tempered with enough water for pressing into brick. Grog, made of the same clay, is added to the mix. Bricks are pressed in a stiff plastic or semi-dry state.

Desirable properties in firebricks are density, strength, well-graded particle size, refractoriness, resistance to spalling and cracking, resistance to acids and slags, and exact sizing. Firebricks are made in four grades or qualities, depending on the degree of temperature they are able to withstand in service. These grades are Superduty (P.C.E. 33), High Heat Duty (P.C.E. 31½), Medium Heat Duty (P.C.E. 29), and Low Heat Duty (P.C.E. 15). (P.C.E. here signifies "pyrometric cone equivalent," or the cone at which the brick would soften.) Bricks designated "Low Heat Duty" are made for use in boilers, fireplaces, and other applications where

MELTING POINTS OF REFRACTORY SUBSTANCES

	Oxides	Carbides	Nitrides	Elements
°C				
4500				
4000				
		Tantalum Carbide 3880		
		Hafnium Carbide 3530		
3500				Carbon 3500
				Tungsten 3370
			Hafnium Nitride 3310	
			Tantalum Nitride 3090	
	ThO₂ 3030			
3000			Zirconium Nitride 2980	Tantalum 2850
	MgO 2800			
	ZrO 2750			
	CaO 2570			
2500	ZrO₂·SiO₂ 2500			
	SrO 2430			
				Iridium 2350
	MgO·Al₂O₃ 2135		Aluminum Nitride 2150	
	Al₂O₃ 2050			
2000	3Al₂O₃·2SiO₂ 1810			
	SiO₂ 1710			

82. *Melting points of refractory substances.*

the heat stress in use is rather mild. For kiln building, "High Heat Duty" bricks should be chosen.

The advantages of hard firebrick for kiln construction are obvious. They are refractory and will serve beyond the highest temperatures ordinarily used for ceramic work. They are hard, dense, and resistant to wear and abrasion. They resist spalling and cracking, and they do not crumble or disintegrate, an especially important property in the crown of the kiln. Furthermore, they are relatively cheap and easily available, and may be obtained in a number of special shapes which facilitate kiln construction. Firebricks are good insulators, although their insulating properties are considerably below that of materials made especially for this purpose.

Figure 83 illustrates the various shapes which are regularly furnished by manufacturers of firebricks. These shapes are standard. The basic shape is the "9 inch straight." The 9 inch series includes only shapes which are 9 inches long. The versatility of this series in the construction of arches, walls and domes will be evident. Larger shapes are also furnished, the most useful of which is perhaps the 9 x 6¾ x 2½. A size tolerance of plus or minus 2% is followed by the manufacturers.

If a kiln is to be used only for low temperature firing, it is possible to construct it of common red brick or buff building brick. But since the use of common brick limits the usefulness of the kiln, it is advisable to use firebrick, and in almost every case the additional cost is justified.

There are a few other natural refractory materials besides clay bricks which can be used for kilns, but each has serious drawbacks compared to clay bricks. High-alumina materials such as silimanite or fused alumina are very refractory, but they are expensive and ordinarily are used only where the chemical properties of alumina are essential, as in the glass and cement industries. Refractory bricks are also made from chromite or magnesite. These chemically basic materials are useful in the steel industry because they resist the slagging action of molten metals. However, they have inferior insulating properties and tend to crack and spall because of high expansion on heating. Bricks made from silica are also used in the steel industry. These may be 90% SiO_2 and are thus highly refractory, but their expansion and contraction on heating and cooling create instability in any masonry structure.

What of natural rocks? One might think that the rocks of the eternal hills would be suitable for kiln construction, but such is not the case. Many rocks are radically altered by heating. Limestone, for example, breaks down into carbon dioxide and quicklime at a very low temperature (about 800° C.) and granite breaks down because of the disintegration of the mica as it is dehydrated, and because of the fusion of the feldspar. Flint cracks up from excessive expansion. Feldspar begins to melt at about cone 6. Shales blow up as combined water violently escapes. Besides clay, the only natural mineral which can be pressed into service for kiln building is sandstone. Sandstone was in fact used in colonial times for iron smelting furnaces and to some extent for kilns. It is refractory, but on heating and cooling

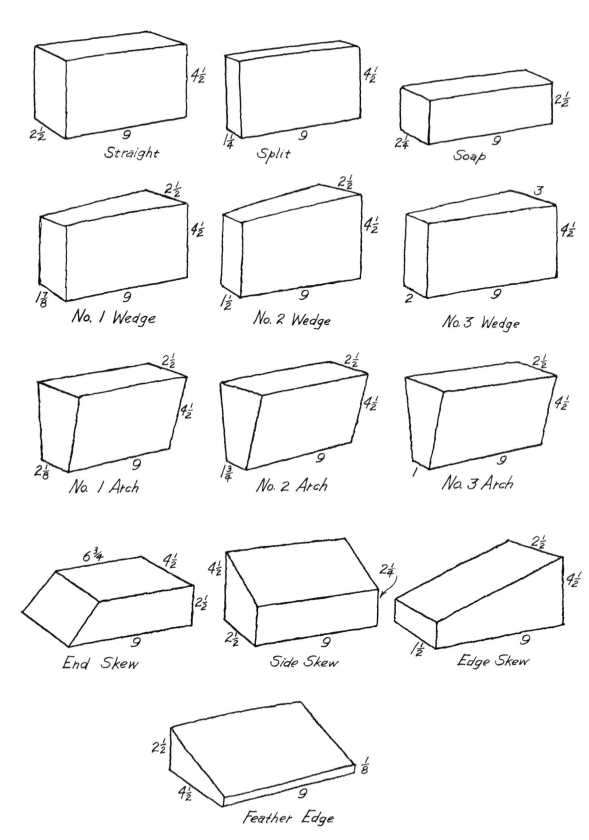

83. *Standard firebrick shapes.*

it tends to crack and disintegrate. Some sandstones, called "firestone," work better than others. The use of sandstone for furnaces was largely discontinued as soon as firebrick became available.

In America, industrial development was seriously hampered until firebrick began to be produced in New Jersey about 1725. With the availability of firebrick, the colonial smiths were no longer dependent on the mother country for iron and steel. It might almost be said that the Revolution was made possible by firebrick—firebrick in which iron could be smelted, from which steel could be forged, from which rifles could be made. Colonial potters often made their own bricks for their first kilns, digging out the clay, forming it in wooden molds and firing in scove kilns.

Refractory blocks, slabs, skewbacks, arches, or door blocks may be made on the job using castable materials. In fact, it is possible to make the whole kiln from a castable material. Refractory castable mixtures are made from a suitable aggregate, such as firebrick grog, insulating firebrick granules, vermiculite, or perlite bonded with calcium aluminate cement. Calcium aluminate cement is similar to portland cement, and when mixed with water will set up in a hard, solid mass. But unlike portland cement, it is refractory and may be heated to red heat or higher without exploding or melting. Most brands of calcium aluminate cement may be used at temperatures in excess of 1300° C.

To cast a shape, a form must first be made. Forms may be made of wood or plywood, securely fastened at the corners, or in the case of curving forms, of bent plywood or masonite suitably reinforced. The forms may be given a light coat of grease to prevent sticking. The aggregate is prepared by crushing old firebrick or fragments of used insulating firebrick. The aggregate should be made up of particles of various sizes, from about $\frac{1}{4}$ inch in diameter to grains as small as sand or smaller. The proportion of very fine particles should not be too great, however. The aggregate is then mixed dry with $\frac{1}{8}$ of its volume of cement. Water is added to this, and the mass is mixed in a mortar box until it is of plastic consistency. It should be well moistened, but not so wet as to flow. The mixture is then shoveled into the mold and rammed into place so as to leave no air pockets. The material will set in a few hours and may then be removed from the mold and cured in a cool place for several days. When thoroughly dry, cast shapes may be incorporated into the kiln structure.

In use, cast refractories become fired on the face which is exposed to the inside of the kiln, while the part which is away from the heat may retain strength from the chemical bond of the cement. Such cast shapes may give excellent service and long life. The only disadvantage is a zone of weakness between the fired portion of the shape and the unfired part, which can cause splitting or spalling. To obviate this difficulty, the shapes may be prefired in a kiln to cone 7 or 8, in which case the cast refractory is similar to one made by pressing and firing fireclay and grog in the usual manner.

It is a tempting idea to cast all the parts of the kiln, including the arch, but certain practical considerations usually rule this out. The aggregate is rather hard to come by, and even if used bricks are available for crushing, this will be a difficult job without the proper machinery. Furthermore, calcium aluminate cement is expensive, and if the forms to be cast are bulky, the cost of the cement may be considerable. Another disadvantage is the great weight of the cast pieces, making them difficult to move and assemble. Of course the parts of a kiln may be cast right in place. The arch, for example, may be cast over a stout wooden form which, when removed, will leave the arch in place and resting on the kiln walls. Cast monolithic arches will require less bracing than arches made up of individual brick units. When all the factors are considered, the kiln builder will usually decide on conventional brick construction. But for special shapes such as skewbacks, pieces forming the transition from square brick chimneys to round metal stacks, and door blocks, cast refractories may be ideal.

Refractory manufacturers sell a plastic firebrick material which can be formed into any shape and used for construction or repair. Such material is a well sized and mixed combination of grog and raw clay, sometimes with sodium silicate added. It is shipped in waterproof bags. This plastic material, essentially stiff, grogged clay, may be rammed into molds, or used to patch parts of the kiln which have deteriorated from long use.

In addition to the "hard" firebrick, "soft" or insulating firebricks are also available. They are a more recent development, coming into general use during the 1930's. Insulating bricks are designed specifically for greater heat retention. There are two kinds of soft insulating brick, those made from the natural material, diatomaceous earth, or Fuller's earth, and those made from clay. Diatomaceous earth bricks are made from the natural deposits of the diatom, a small sea animal whose myriad shells have formed thick marine deposits. The material is soft, light, porous, and consists largely of silicon dioxide. Bricks can be made from quarried diatomaceous earth, cut and sized to shape, or diatomaceous earth can be mixed with a little clay, pressed into bricks and fired. The multitude of air cells in the material forms an effective heat barrier. Diatomaceous earth bricks have the drawback of being rather weak in structure and are not highly refractory. They are used as backup insulation behind other types of bricks.

Clay insulating bricks are made from refractory fireclays and kaolins. The clay is mixed into a heavy slip into which air bubbles are induced by chemical means. When the material is set and dried, it is fired and later cut and shaped into sized bricks. The entrapped air pockets make a light, porous brick, with high insulating properties and, if made from the proper clay, excellent resistance to heat. Porous bricks are also made by mixing wood fragments with the clay. Bricks are graded according to "K factors" and those sold as "K-30," for example, will withstand 3000° F. without melting, bloating or deformation. Other common grades are K-28,

K-26, K-23, K-20 and K-16, serviceable at 2800°, 2600°, 2300°, 2000° and 1600° F. respectively.

Insulating bricks serve to increase the heat retention properties of kilns. They may be used as a backup layer behind regular hard firebrick, or they may be used for the entire kiln structure. Their use has revolutionized the design of kilns and furnaces of all sorts. The initial costs of insulating bricks is high, but this initial investment may be retrieved in lowered firing costs over a period of time.

The table in Figure 84 shows the relative conductivity of various insulating firebrick compared to firebrick. It will be noted that the lower grades of insulating

PROPERTIES OF INSULATING BRICK

	K-23	K-26	K-28	HIGH HEAT DUTY FIREBRICK
True porosity, %	70	70	70	22
Density, lbs./ft.³	48	48	48	
Cold crushing strength, lb./sq. in.	270	350	600	
Maximum service temperature, °C,	1260	1450	1538	1550
Thermal conductivity * at mean temperature of:				
400° C.	2.13	2.18	2.89	
600° C.	2.37	2.36	3.12	
800° C.	2.63	2.57	3.39	
1000° C.		2.80	3.70	

* B.t.u.—in.ft.$^{-2}$ F^{-1}hr.$^{-1}$

84. *Properties of insulating firebrick.*

firebrick, while less refractory, are more effective insulators. As shown in the chart in Figure 85, the K-23 brick has a heat loss of 297 B.t.u.'s as compared to 609 B.t.u.'s for the K-30 brick and 1675 B.t.u.'s for the hard firebrick. At this furnace temperature, the K-23 brick is over five times more effective in insulating property than the hard firebrick. Most of the higher insulating properties in insulating bricks are due to the presence of entrapped voids in the structure. Heat travels with difficulty in air or gas alone. The loose association of the particles also impedes the flow of heat by conduction. Insulating bricks are so effective that a brick which is heated up to red heat on one end can easily be picked up in the hand at the other end.

The chart in Figure 85 also shows the marked difference in heat storage capacity between the various grades of insulation brick and firebrick. Whereas a K-23 brick has a heat storage capacity of 6000 B.t.u.'s, a hard firebrick has a capacity of over five times that amount. This means that the hard firebrick can actually soak up more heat and will take that much longer to cool. If a kiln is made of hard firebricks only, much more heat will be required just to heat up the kiln itself, and fuel costs will be higher, even disregarding the loss of heat through the wall of the kiln.

85. *Heat loss and heat storage in a 9-inch wall with hot-face temperature held at 2200° F.*

	HEAT LOSS in B.t.u./(sq.ft.) (hr.)	HEAT STORAGE CAPACITY B.t.u. per sq. ft.
K-23 Brick	297	6000
K-26 Brick	492	8000
K-28 Brick	507	8300
K-30 Brick	609	10,800
Firebrick	1675	30,500

The decision as to whether to use insulating bricks for the construction of part or the whole of a ceramic kiln is largely a matter of economics. The use of insulation in no way improves the product being fired. It is purely a matter of savings in fuel, and of whether the higher cost of insulating bricks will, in time, be offset by the lower cost of firing. If insulating bricks are used for the inside face of the kiln, an additional factor must be taken into consideration, i.e., the shorter life of soft bricks relative to hard firebrick.

Besides insulating firebrick, there are a few other materials that can be used for insulating kilns. Vermiculite, especially, is very useful. It is cheap and readily available from building supply dealers. It is an expanded mica with a very loose structure yielding innumerable air spaces which impede the flow of heat. Vermiculite can be used as a loose fill over the arch of the kiln, or it may be poured into cavities between the inner and outer wall of the kiln. Another possibility is to form a plaster of vermiculite and clay which can be built up on the outer walls or top of the kiln. A good mixture is 85 parts by weight of vermiculite and 15 parts of ball clay. The mixture is wet just sufficiently to make a thick plaster. Sodium silicate may be added to give the material strength when it dries. About one quart of sodium silicate to each 100 pounds of dry mix will be enough to give some toughness to the insulation. Or, bricks can be formed of vermiculite, clay, and sodium silicate, and when dry, these may be used as backup insulation on the walls or crown of the kiln. Since vermiculite is not highly refractory, it cannot be used to form the interior wall of the kiln, but it serves well as a second layer and has high insulating value. Obviously, where structural strength is required, vermiculite is not practical because of the weak structure of the particles.

Another insulator already mentioned is diatomaceous earth. This may be purchased as a loose material and used to fill wall cavities or placed above arches.

Asbestos board or asbestos plaster is sometimes used for kiln insulation. Like vermiculite, it is not highly refractory and can be used only for the outside walls of the kiln. But its insulation value is high and if used as slabs or boards on the outside of the kiln it will serve well as a heat barrier. Fiberglas or feldspathic wool may also be used in areas not subjected to high temperatures. Raw clay itself may be used for insulation. In the past it was common practice to plaster the outside of the kiln with clay, sometimes mixed with chopped straw or grass. This coating served to chink up the cracks and also to insulate. Another possibility is a mixture of clay and ashes applied to the outside of the kiln as a plaster, or used as an insulating fill. Actually, raw clay or a mixture of clay and grog works quite well as an insulating fill, but it is not as efficient as vermiculite. Another possible insulating material is ground charcoal. This may seem improbable because of the likelihood of its burning, but if mixed into a paste with raw clay and used in spots where air does not reach it, it is quite an efficient insulator, and is of course highly refractory.

Aluminum foil is a useful insulating material. Its reflectant surface will deflect and throw back radiant heat. If a layer of foil is placed between the inner and outer courses of a kiln wall, it will serve to deflect part of the heat back toward the inner wall, and will prevent the escape of some of the heat which would otherwise penetrate the wall by radiation.

Firebricks may fail in three ways:

(1) They may melt or deform from excessive heat, or be corroded by materials coming into contact with them, such as slags or metals. Failure of this kind seldom occurs in pottery kilns, where the operating temperature is usually far below the melting point of the refractories and where no corrosive materials are being fired.

(2) Bricks may crack or spall. When a brick is heated more at one end than the other, as is usually the case in a kiln, a strain is set up because of the greater expansion in the hotter part. This may cause the brick to break, or a portion of it to flake off (spall), especially if the heating and cooling cycle is rapid. Since pottery kilns are usually heated and cooled rather slowly, the bricks are not subjected to severe shock and tend to have a long life.

(3) Bricks may crumble from fatigue. Repeated heating and cooling loosens the bond between the particles and the bricks gradually lose their original strength.

3

Heat Retention
and Transfer

As it developed historically, and as it essentially exists today, the kiln is a box of refractory material which accumulates and retains the heat directed into it. A consideration of how heat is transferred from one body to another will help to clarify the operation of the kiln.

Heat may be transferred by one of three mechanisms: conduction, convection, or radiation. In the conduction of heat through a solid, the increased molecular activity caused by temperature elevation is transferred from one molecule to the other, thus spreading through the body that is being heated. In a solid heat travels from regions of high temperature to regions of low temperature. As noted in the section above, different substances differ greatly in their ability to conduct heat. The quantity of heat that passes by conduction through a barrier depends upon several variables:

1. The area of the conducting surface. The larger the area the more heat that is carried.
2. The thickness of the conducting material.
3. The difference in temperature between the two sides of the conducting solid.
4. The time allowed for transfer.
5. The nature of the material.

The factor of conductivity is expressed by the value K, which equals B.t.u.'s transmitted per hour through a thickness of one inch and an area of 1 square foot for a temperature difference of 1 degree Fahrenheit. The K factor of silver, for example, is 1715. It is one of the best conductors. But the factor of an insulating firebrick is only about 3. There is a vast difference in the ability of these two materials to transmit heat by conduction.

The second way in which heat can be transferred is by convection. In this case a liquid or a gas moves because it has become heated, and transfers its heat to something else. An actual movement of matter takes place. In the case of kilns, convection occurs when hot gases travel through a kiln, transferring some of their heat to the surfaces contacted.

The third way in which heat is transferred from one body to another is by radiation. Heat generates electromagnetic waves which travel through space by mechanisms as yet little understood.

All three of these mechanisms by which heat is transferred from one substance to another have important application in kiln design. The rate of conduction through the walls of the kiln governs the rate of heat loss, and hence the ability of the kiln to serve as a reservoir of heat. Even if metal were sufficiently refractory to withstand high temperatures, it would be useless as a material for the walls of kilns because it would transmit heat too rapidly to the outside. Insulating firebricks, on the other hand, are highly efficient and retain heat remarkably well.

Heat is spread through the interior of the kiln by convection and radiation. When fuel is burned in a kiln, a flow of hot gases is induced, passing through and finally out of the kiln. These hot gases consist of unburned air, carbon dioxide (CO_2), carbon monoxide (CO), and nitrogen gas. As these hot gases course through the objects in the kiln, they give up some of their heat by contact with the cooler surfaces. The faster the gases travel over cooler surfaces, the more heat they are able to transfer.

Obviously, if the kiln is to extract the maximum amount of heat by convection of the hot gases originating in combustion, there must be good circulation to all parts of the kiln, and the ware chamber and its contents must not be too far from the source of heat.

While convection is the most important mechanism of heat transfer in kilns, heat is also transmitted to all parts of the kiln inside by radiation. When the areas near the source of heat become incandescent, these areas give off heat by radiation to other surfaces. Heat travels from one surface and from one object to another in this manner. The presence of ware inside the kiln, with its many reflectant surfaces, facilitates radiation. Kilns which are filled with ware may heat up more evenly and efficiently than when empty. Smooth, white surfaces will radiate heat more effectively than dark colored, rough surfaces.

It might be thought that thicker-walled kilns would be more efficient. This is not necessarily the case. The walls of the kiln absorb quantities of heat, and if the firing is not of excessive duration, it is completed before the walls of the kiln have become heated to capacity. In this case, thicker walls serve no purpose and only slow down cooling. But for extended firing, thick walls might be desirable. For most pottery firing, a 9-inch kiln wall of hard firebrick is adequate, and a wall $4\frac{1}{2}''$ thick may be sufficient if K-23 or K-26 insulating bricks are used. Japanese chamber kilns are often no more than $6''$ thick and yet serve efficiently in the short firing cycle employed.

4

Masonry
Construction

SINCE POTTERY KILNS are fairly simple structures, usually
no great difficulty is encountered in their construction. A little common sense, and
some knowledge of bricklaying technique is all that is required.

Like all building structures, the kiln must have a suitable foundation. If built
indoors it should have a reinforced concrete foundation at least $3\frac{1}{2}''$ thick, or be
built on a solid floor. If constructed outside in northern latitudes where the ground
freezes, it should have footers going down below the frost line. These can be constructed of concrete, concrete block, or stone. Foundations need be built only for
bearing walls and for the chimney. If the chimney is to be large, a good foundation is especially important to prevent leaning. While a "leaning tower of Pisa" in
the backyard might excite interest, it would be a hazard, especially during firing.
Foundations must be leveled off true for the start of masonry construction.

Small kilns are often built on a platform to bring the door height up to a more
convenient level. This understructure can be built of concrete blocks, red brick,
or stone, using regular cement mortar. In some cases, small kilns may be built on
steel frames provided with casters for mobility. Firebrick walls are built by laying
up the bricks with a thin layer of fireclay mortar between them. The best mortar
for kilns is composed of about two parts fireclay and one part grog or sand, preferably grog. This is mixed with water with a hoe in a mason's wooden mortar box,
and should be the consistency of soft mud, almost soft enough to flow. For better
dry strength, liquid sodium silicate may be added, about 1 quart per 100 lbs. of dry
mortar. Commercially prepared fireclay mortars usually contain sodium silicate
but it is not really necessary in most cases. These are carefully prepared and pro-
portioned and give good results, but homemade mortars will serve just as well and
are cheaper.

The important thing in building a brick wall is to keep the structure level and plumb. To achieve this, each brick must be carefully placed and moved, or tapped with the hammer or trowel until it lines up perfectly with the rest of the structure. Amateur bricklayers invariably allow little irregularities to creep into the work, thinking that they can make sufficient adjustment with the next course to make things true. But usually, the farther one goes the more irregular the wall becomes. Although a professional mason may seem finicky in his attention to the positioning of each brick, this manner of working proves to be the most efficient in the long run. The sum of many well layed bricks will be a well made structure, straight and true.

Bricks are layed in alternating patterns so that joints are "broken." This gives an effective tie between bricks because of the overlapping and prevents the alignment of joints. Figure 86 shows some of the possibilities. In a wall only one brick thick, the joints are staggered. In a wall two bricks thick, stretcher courses are alternated

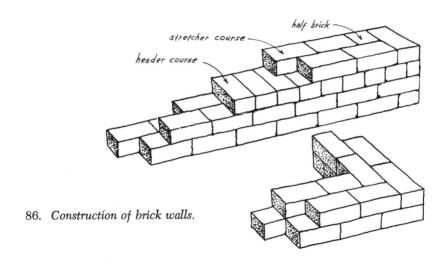

86.   *Construction of brick walls.*

with header courses, making a solid wall. Some amateurs fear to build a kiln because they can find no plan that gives the position of *each* brick, but such detailing is entirely unnecessary. Common sense will guide the mason to lay the bricks so that the joints coincide as little as possible and so the bricks overlap for maximum strength. That is the basic principle for a good brick wall.

It will be seen that breaking the joints will necessitate the use of half bricks in some places, or even smaller pieces, and usually it is necessary to cut some bricks. Professional masons use a power brick saw for this purpose, but cutting may be satisfactorily done by hand. To cut a hard firebrick, it is scored around by sharp taps with the claw of the brick hammer, especially at the corners. The brick may

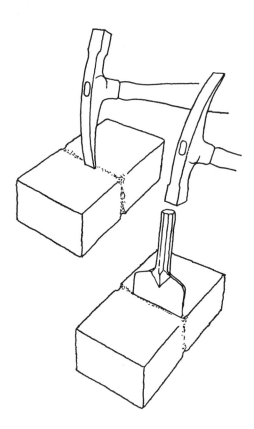

87. *Method of cutting a firebrick.*

then be placed on a soft surface, such as a piece of old blanket or a bed of sand, and broken with a sharp blow of the brick set and hammer as shown in Figure 87.

In laying firebricks, only a small amount of clay mortar is used. The purpose of the mortar is not to stick the bricks together, but rather to level them up and to provide a solid bed for each brick. The mortar also serves to fill the cracks and makes for a more airtight structure. The mortar can be applied either by dipping the bricks into it, or by application with the trowel. At the job, mortar is kept on a mortar board, from which it may be conveniently lifted with the trowel. The bricks should be dampened. If the bricks are layed dry, they will suck the water out of the mortar quickly, and it will be impossible to tap the brick into position. Most amateurs have a tendency to work with mortar which is too stiff, and they consequently have great difficulty in tapping the bricks into alignment. Dampened bricks and a loose mortar makes the work of correctly placing each brick much easier. Firebricks are relatively uniform in size, so there is no need to use thick layers of mortar to compensate for irregularities in the brick, as is the case in construction with common red building brick.

Expansion joints must be provided in the brickwork of kilns. If no expansion space is provided for, the kiln will bulge and swell on heating due to the expansion of the bricks. In practice, a space of about $\frac{1}{4}$ inch is allowed between the ends of every third or fourth brick. This space should not be filled with mortar. More space than this is sometimes allowed just to be sure that the wall will not be too tight.

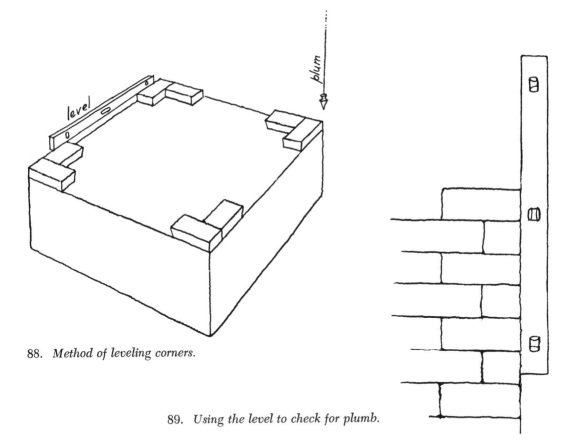

88. *Method of leveling corners.*

89. *Using the level to check for plumb.*

In kiln building it is much better to have a loose structure than a tight one. For this reason the amateur may have a slight advantage over the professional mason, because his bricklaying is apt to be somewhat loose and not tightly locked together. I have seen kilns made by professional bricklayers which in use suffered severe cracking and swelling due to the overly tight and precise workmanship and the lack of expansion joints.

To make a rectangular structure of brick, level corners are established first. It is especially important to get the corners level from the start. One layer of brick is then laid at the corners, as shown in Figure 88. After the corners are established, bricks are added to complete the course all around. String may be stretched from one corner to the other to guide the alignment of bricks, or the level may be used. The next course is started in the same way. This second course is checked for plumb as shown in Figure 89. It is important to check each brick for plumb as it is layed, and it is better to use the level rather than depend on the eye. Bricklaying is like playing with blocks, although somewhat more complicated, especially when it comes to doors, openings and arches. If the design is conceived in terms of the multiples of the size of bricks the actual work is facilitated because there is less brick cutting. If a firebrick inner wall is backed up on the outside with red bricks, the red bricks can be layed up at the same time, using cement mortar. Red bricks are ½ inch narrower than firebrick and 1 inch shorter, but this difference can be made up with a thicker mortar joint, which is normal in common brick walls. An

90. *Kiln built by Don Reitz in Spring Green, Wisconsin. The wall is completed to a point above the burner ports and flue.*

91. *Don Reitz kiln. The arch form is removed.*

92. *Basic form of the kiln is complete.*

93. *Don Reitz kiln firing on liquified petroleum gas. A second layer of brick has been added to the side walls and arch.*

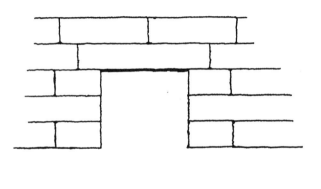

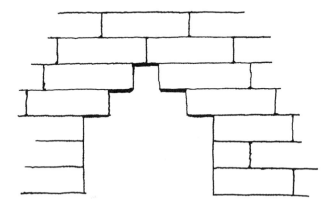

94. *Lintel and corbel arch.*

occassional tie with a firebrick extending into the red brick will bind the two walls together. Sometimes a double wall of this kind is made, allowing for a narrow space of about one inch between walls. This is packed full of vermiculite as construction proceeds. Or, a sandwich of insulating brick between hard firebrick and the red brick may complete the wall.

While straight walls are easy to build, arches over flue holes, doors, and crowns are more of a problem. To bridge over small openings such as burner ports, a brick is used as a lintel. This will serve to bridge over holes up to six inches across. For larger openings, the corbel arch may be used, as shown in Figure 94. Here, the opening is narrowed a bit with each course, until it may be spanned with one brick. Corbel arches are not practical for openings more than about 18 inches across. Sometimes special shapes longer than nine inches are used to form a lintel over openings.

The arch is a beautiful structure and a pleasure to build. Figure 95 shows its features: A is the span, B is the rise, C is the radius, D is the skewback, and E is the buttress. Although the arch is self-supporting, it exerts a thrust against the skewback which must be countered by a buttress or a brace.

The most stable arches for ceramic kilns are of fairly low rise. The barrel vault or round arch is not recommended. There is no hard and fast rule governing the relationship of the rise to the span of the arch, but most arches used in kilns have a span which subtends about 60° of the circle. The rise may vary from about one inch per foot of span, which is a flat arch, to about two-and-one-half inches rise per foot of a span. Preliminary to construction, the arch can be laid out on a large sheet of paper. With the rise and span determined, the radius can be determined experimentally with a compass made from a pencil, string, and a pin. Extensions of the radius lines determine the slope of the skewback.

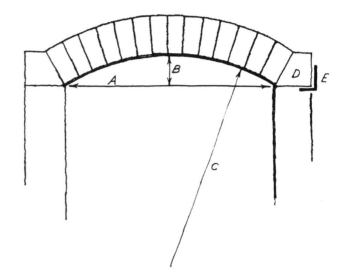

95. *Features of the arch.*

To determine the number and shape of brick to span the arch, cardboard templates can be cut the size of the various arch bricks, #1, #2, or #3 (see brick size chart). These cardboard templates are then tried out on a full size drawing of the arch, and a combination of the various shapes, including straights, is found that will form the arch. It may not be possible to get an exact fit, but the mortar between the bricks will compensate. Straights and splits should be used as little as possible, because, not being keyed in, they tend to drop down with repeated firings. Figure 96 shows arches of various span and rise and the number and kind of arch brick needed to build them. Arches may be either four-and-one-half inches thick, in which case arch bricks are used, or they may be nine inches thick and made up of wedge brick. Skewbacks can be bought ready made, as shown in Figure 97, but it is not hard to cut them to the proper angle with the brick hammer. Small irregularities are made up with a bed of mortar plastered on the skewback.

To determine the number and kind of brick to complete one course of an arch of any given span and rise, the following calculation may be used.

1. Determine the inclosed angle θ and the radius, R, as shown in Figure 98.
2. From the radius, calculate the circumferance of the circles C-1 and C-2, using the formula $C = 2\pi R$.

4½ ARCH THICKNESS—1½ INCH RISE PER FOOT OF SPAN

Span	Rise	Inside Radius	Number of bricks required per course			
			No. 2 Arch	No. 1 Arch	Straight	Total
1'—0''	1½''	1'—0¾''	5	2	"	7
1'—6''	2¼''	1'—7⅛''	3	7	"	10
2'—0''	3''	2'—1½''	"	12	"	12
2'—6''	3¾''	2'—7⅞''	"	12	3	15
3'—0''	4½''	3'—2¼''	"	12	5	17
3'—6''	5¼''	3'—8⅝''	"	12	8	20
4'—0''	6''	4'—3''	"	12	10	22
4'—6''	6¾''	4'—9⅜''	"	12	13	25
5'—0''	7½''	5'—3¾''	"	12	15	27
5'—6''	8¼''	5'—10⅛''	"	12	18	30
6'—0''	9''	6'—4½''	"	12	20	32

9'' ARCH THICKNESS 2⁵⁄₁₆'' RISE PER FOOT OF SPAN

Span	Rise	Inside Radius	Number of bricks required per course			
			No. 2 Wedge	No. 1 Wedge	No.1-X Wedge*	Total
1'—6''	3¹⁵⁄₃₂''	1'—1¹⁵⁄₃₂''	14	"	"	14
2'—0''	4¹⁹⁄₃₂''	1'—5¹⁵⁄₁₆''	9	7	"	16
2'—6''	5¾''	1'—10⁷⁄₁₆''	5	14	"	19
3'—0''	6²⁹⁄₃₂''	2'—2²⁹⁄₃₂''	"	21	"	21
3'—6''	8¹⁄₁₆''	2'—7¹³⁄₃₂''	"	20	4	24
4'—0''	9⁷⁄₃₂''	2'—11⅞''	"	18	9	27
4'—6''	10⅜''	3'—4⅜''	"	16	13	29
5'—0''	11½''	3'—8²⁷⁄₃₂''	"	14	18	32
5'—6''	1'—0²¹⁄₃₂''	4'—1¹¹⁄₃₂''	"	13	22	35
6'—0''	1'—1¹³⁄₁₆''	4'—5¹³⁄₁₆''	"	11	26	37

* Note: No. 1-X Wedge Brick measures 9'' x 4½'' x (2½''–2¼'').

96. *Table of bricks required to form arches of various spans.*

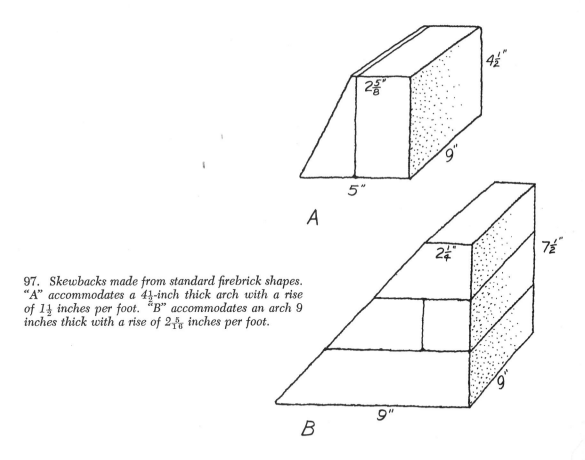

97. *Skewbacks made from standard firebrick shapes. "A" accommodates a 4½-inch thick arch with a rise of 1½ inches per foot. "B" accommodates an arch 9 inches thick with a rise of $2\frac{5}{16}$ inches per foot.*

3. Divide 360 into θ. This gives the percentage of the circumference occupied by arcs *A-1* and *A-2*.
4. Find the actual length of *A-1* and *A-2* by multiplying the percentage figure found above by the circumference.
5. Divide the length of *A-1* by 2½. This gives the number of brick required.
6. Subtract *A-2* from *A-1*. This gives the total taper required.
7. Divide the taper of a single brick into the total taper. This gives the number of tapered brick required. The rest of the brick may be straights.

If the kiln builder does not feel up to this calculation he can proceed with the cut-and-try method, using cardboard templates as indicated above.

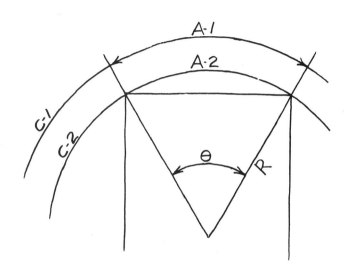

98. *Calculation of arch brick.*

99. *Two-chamber kiln designed by Paul Soldner. The kiln is fired with burners entering a firebox under the door. The second chamber, a tall parabola form, functions as a stack to induce draft in the first chamber.*

100. *Kiln designed and built by Michael and Harriet Cohen at New Ipswich, N. H. The kiln is a catenary arch form.*

101. *Harriet Cohen setting the car.*

102. *Michael Cohen adjusts the burners of the kiln. Each burner has a pressure gauge which gives an accurate reading of the amount of gas being used.*

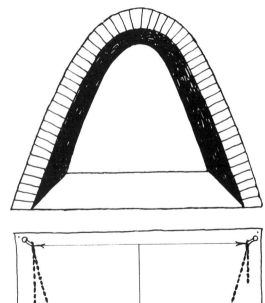

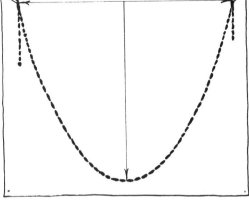

103. *The catenary arch.*

A form must be built to hold up the arch during construction. This can be made of wood, as shown in Figure 104. The top of the form is propped up in the kiln, using wedges to raise it to just the proper height. Then the arch is built, starting from the two sides and working toward the middle. As in wall construction, joints

104. *Wooden arch form.*

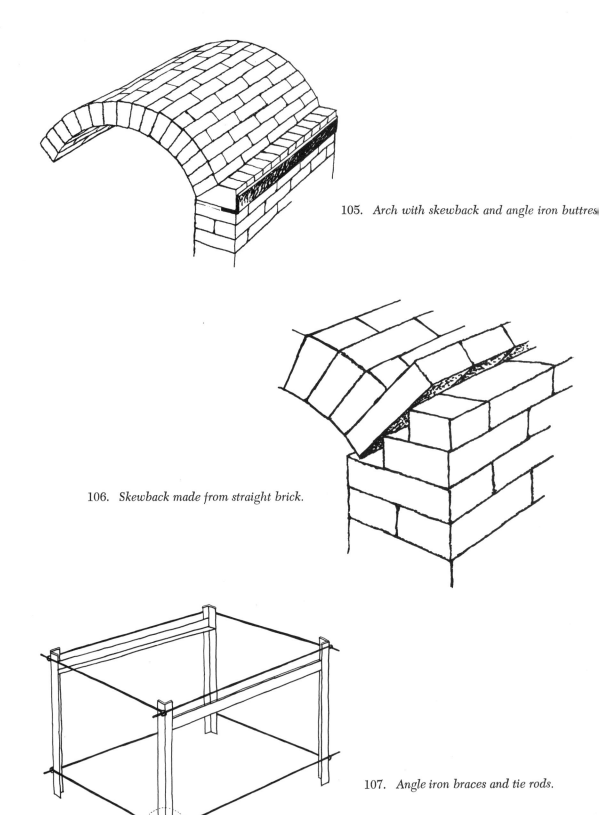

105. *Arch with skewback and angle iron buttress*

106. *Skewback made from straight brick.*

107. *Angle iron braces and tie rods.*

are broken, as shown in Figure 105. The center course should fit snugly. Enough mortar is used to give a good bearing on all the bricks. The center course is tapped down into place with a brick hammer and a piece of wood. When the arch is completed, the wooden form may be withdrawn.

To absorb the thrust of the arch, metal bracing is used on the outside of the kiln. A steel angle iron is inserted just behind the skewback to hold it securely in place, as shown in Figure 105. Angle irons are placed at the corners to hold the skewback support. Metal tie rods are used to hold the corner braces in place. For small kilns, 2 x 2 inch angle iron is sufficient, and $\frac{1}{2}$ inch tie rods are suitable. Tie rods are secured as shown in Figure 107. The metal bracing on small kilns is intended only to carry the thrust of the arch and is not needed to hold the walls in place. It need not be screwed up tightly. Sometimes lock-nuts or springs are used to take up expansion which occurs when the kiln is heated. In large kilns, channel iron braces called buckstays are placed upright at the sides of the kiln to counter the thrust of the arch, and these are usually tied together with rods passing over the top of the kiln.

The catenary arch, Figure 104, is a beautiful structure and very useful in kiln building. The catenary is related to the parabaloid curve, and can be calculated mathematically, but in practice it is determined by hanging a chain on a wall suspended from two points, allowing it to drape down naturally in a curve. The curve of the chain can be traced off onto a large piece of paper and used as a guide for making the arch form. If the catenary arch is too wide, or too tall, it will be relatively unstable. An arch which is about as high as it is wide is the most stable. The great advantage of the catenary arch is that it exerts its thrust downward and requires no buttressing. In kiln building, this means that there is no need for exterior bracing or support. There is also an advantage in the catenary arch's being one complete structure embracing walls and crown. Less surface is required to enclose a given volume than is the case with a structure composed of walls and arch.

When expansion occurs, the stress is evenly divided throughout the arch. The shape of the arch is easily adapted to various kiln designs. The end walls that complete the enclosure may be built either under the arch, or outside the arch. The former system is better, because walls built outside the arch must be pressed against it by some sort of external bracing. Catenary arches may be made from arch bricks if a $4\frac{1}{2}$-inch thickness is adequate, or from wedge brick for a thickness of 9 inches. Or, a $4\frac{1}{2}$-inch catenary arch may be topped with a layer of insulating bricks $2\frac{1}{4}$ or $4\frac{1}{2}$ inches thick. It is not advisable to build catenary arches of two distinct layers of hard bricks, because the upper arch, instead of adding strength, will merely rest on the lower one when the latter is expanded from heat. Catenary arches may be built entirely of straight bricks, the crevices at the outside being filled with clay, but whenever possible, shaped brick should be used for permanence.

Corner braces of angle iron and tie rods are usually all that are required to stabilize the structure of the kiln and to minimize the effects of expansion. Expan-

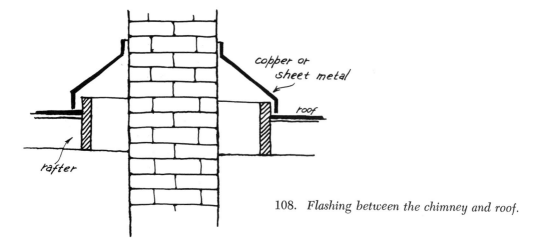

108. *Flashing between the chimney and roof.*

sion cannot be prevented, but it can be allowed for. If the brickwork is provided with expansion joints and the masonry is not too tight, there is an opportunity for each brick to move a little, independently, and the entire structure will not be subject to undue strain.

The sides and jambs of kiln doors should be built with hard firebrick. It is best to arch over the door. This is done in the same way as the main arch is built. A wooden form is constructed to hold up the arch during construction, and skewbacks are prepared. The thrust of the door arch is slight compared to the main arch over the kiln, and the mass of the walls furnishes sufficient buttress.

Chimneys are built using the same masonry techniques. It is well to dimension the chimney in multiples of bricks. Thus the outside might be $13\frac{1}{2}$ x $13\frac{1}{2}$ inches or 18 x 18 inches. Firebrick should be used for the chimney to a height of at least 12 feet. Beyond that, fireclay flue liners with red brick outside may be used.

Where chimneys go through the roof, careful attention must be given to the design of the sleeve or flashing. Figure 108 shows a satisfactory and safe design. The hole in the roof is larger than the chimney by at least 8 inches on all sides, and the brickwork of the chimney does not come in contact with wood at any point. A copper or galvanized iron roof jack gives a weatherproof closure. To solve the problem of the passage of the chimney through a roof it is a good idea to call in a professional roofer or tinsmith. This is not a good place to practice economy since the safety of the building is at stake. Wood-fired kilns will develop a high chimney temperature, and special care must be given to the flashing.

Figure 109 shows some possible wall designs for small kilns. Even if insulating bricks are used, the wall is ordinarily at least $4\frac{1}{2}$ inches thick. However, for small test kilns or kilns for low firing or for Raku, insulating brick laid on edge are sometimes used, giving a wall thickness of only $2\frac{1}{2}$ inches. Two grades of insulating brick make a good wall, or hard firebrick backed up with a low grade insulating brick. For most small kilns a wall thickness of more than 9 inches in unnecessary, but some kiln builders prefer to give the kiln an outer jacket of red brick laid up with cement mortar. This certainly makes a permanent looking structure.

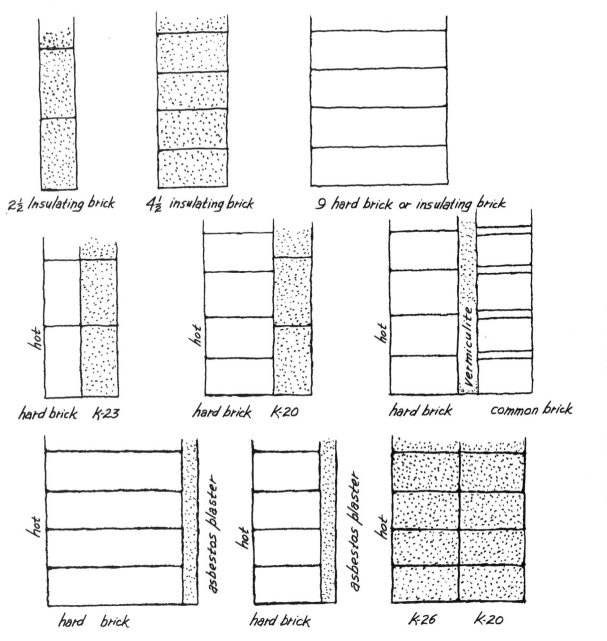

2½ Insulating brick **4½ insulating brick** **9 hard brick or insulating brick**

hot | hard brick K-23

hot | hard brick K-20

hot | hard brick | Vermiculite | common brick

hot | hard brick | asbestos plaster

hot | hard brick | asbestos plaster

hot | K-26 K-20

109. *Some possible kiln wall combinations.*

Soft insulating brick may be handled differently from hard brick, and in most respects building with them is easier. Since insulating brick are made in exact shapes, little or no mortar is required to lay them into walls. If mortar is used, it should be very thin, about the consistency of malted milk. The brick can be dipped into mortar and set in place. If no mortar is used, the brick are just piled up like blocks. Structures of loose brick can be built very quickly. Insulating bricks can be easily cut. The best tool for this is a pruning saw with large teeth. Since the bricks

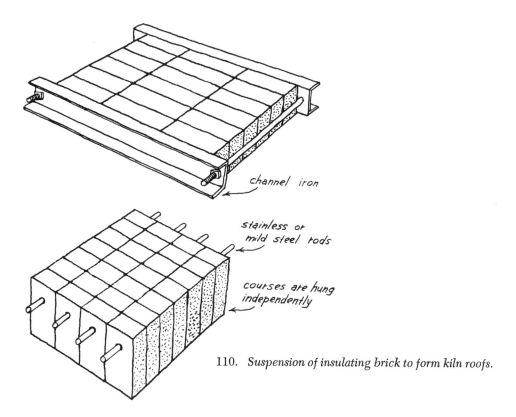

channel iron

stainless or
mild steel rods

courses are hung
independently

110. *Suspension of insulating brick to form kiln roofs.*

are easy to shape, arches can be made by cutting each brick to fit rather than by buying arch bricks already shaped.

Insulating bricks are so light they can be suspended to form flat roofs. Figure 110 shows a roof made of insulating brick which have been drilled and hung on steel rods. The rods are threaded and bolted to exert inward pressure against angle irons which hold the mass of brick together. This style of roof may be used instead of the harder-to-build arch. It is supported by the walls and can be easily removed for repair. Small flat roofs can be made by clamping together a number of insulating brick with the tightened steel strap used for reinforcing shipping cartons. Brick held together this way, however, have a tendency to become loose. The suspended roof may seem like a simple solution. But in use the suspended bricks tend to break off and drop downward into the kiln. The arch structure is actually much more durable. Insulating brick may be used to build semipermanent kiln structures, and if no mortar is used the kiln can later be taken apart and erected again in another location if desired. Or, revisions in size or design may be easily made. In some situations, this flexibility is very desirable. If the kiln is used for any length of time, however, it will be found that tearing it down results in a pile of mostly broken bricks, and rebuilding will entail considerable further expense.

Kilns made entirely of insulating brick have some disadvantages. Although they retain heat efficiently, they cool down quite rapidly because of the low heat capacity of the material. Compared to a hard firebrick, an insulating brick will not soak up nearly as many B.t.u.'s during the fire. If a kiln does cool too fast, a small amount of heat can be fed in from one or more burners during the first part of the cooling cycle. A more serious disadvantage of insulating brick kilns is their relatively poor durability. Because of their soft, porous structure insulating bricks will, in time, crack and crumble. Every refractory is subject to fatigue, caused by the expansion and contraction which attends repeated heating and cooling. Insulating bricks hold up well for many firings, but they reach a point at which much of their original strength is gone. Hard firebrick will outlast them many times over.

The life of insulating firebrick can be prolonged by coating those surfaces which face inside the kiln with a kiln wash. This seals the pores and prevents combustion gases from entering the structure of the brick. Some commercial sealing coatings are available for this purpose and may be obtained from the manufacturers of the bricks. A coating also improves the reflectance of the surface and thus the transfer of radiant heat during firing.

Before deciding to build a kiln with insulating brick, many factors must be considered, such as the initial cost, the permanence of the structure, ease of construction, and even appearance. More and more, builders of small ceramic kilns are deciding in favor of insulating brick structures, even though the initial cost is usually much higher. Ease of construction is usually the deciding factor.

5

Proportions and
Design of the Kiln

"... at one time my work was baked in front and not behind;
the next time, when I tried to prevent such an accident I would burn it behind and the
front would not be baked; sometimes it was cooked on the right and burned on the left;
sometimes my glazes were put on too thin, and sometimes too thick: which caused me
heavy losses: sometimes when I had glazes of various colors in the kiln, some were burned
before the others had melted. In short, I blundered thus for fifteen or sixteen years: when
I had learned to guard against one danger, I encountered another that I would never have
thought about."

Bernard Palissy—1584*

The design and proportioning of kilns is more of an art than a science. There are
mysteries and uncertainties about it, but existing successful kilns are of so many
varied shapes that it would seem that almost any shape would work. Actually, there
is a wide tolerance of design in kilns, and if a few basic principles are followed
the kiln is apt to work well.

The best general shape for a kiln is something approaching a cube. The cube
encloses more space per area of wall than any other rectilinear shape. Obviously,
if the kiln were made very narrow or very flat in shape, more wall area would be
required per cubic foot of content. A compact shape also favors the circulation of
heat, and the exchange of heat through radiation. The kiln may be a bit higher
than it is wide, or longer than it is high, but in general, it is best to have these
dimensions somewhat equal. Kilns are built in rectilinear shapes mostly for convenience in planning and construction, but the cylindrical shape with a dome is
perhaps a better shape for the circulation of heat. However round kilns or beehive

*The Admirable Discourses of Bernard Palissy, edited by Aurele LaRocque (Urbana: University
of Illinois Press, 1957).

designs are seldom built except in the case of very large kilns because of the awkwardness of building curved structures with rectilinear bricks.

Most atmospheric gas burners used on kilns are rated about 150,000 B.t.u.'s. As a rule of thumb, each cubic foot of kiln space requires at least 30,000 B.t.u.'s heating capacity. In updraft kilns it is better to use more burners of less capacity. And in practice it is always best to have some extra capacity in burners rather than too little. The number of burners to use is a problem. It depends on the reserve power of the burners. A kiln of 10 cubic feet is usually fitted with four gas burners, and one of 25 to 40 cubic feet with six. More burners give a better distribution of heat by introducing it at several points. While one oil burner will be enough to heat a 10 cubic foot kiln, two will be better. With wood or coal firing, one large box is preferred, unless the kiln is quite large.

Space must be provided for combustion. In the case of gas, each burner needs an area of about 500 cubic inches ahead of it in which the gas can burn. This means placing the deflecting wall about $4\frac{1}{2}$ inches from the wall of the kiln and providing an empty space where the gas can ignite. Oil will need a somewhat larger space. Since it burns in a longer flame, an unobstructed space ahead of the burner should be allowed for. Wood takes still more space for proper combustion.

Another critical area is the flue. Here it is better to "over-engineer" and provide a flue large enough to accommodate any foreseeable need. A small gas kiln of 10 cubic feet will need a flue hole of about 40 square inches. This dimension is dependent on the number of burners and the height and pull of the stack. Kilns up to 40 cubic feet are usually given a 9″ x 9″ flue, which seems ample in most cases. For burning wood, a larger flue must be provided. The chimney height may vary from 6 or 8 feet to 30 feet, depending on the size of the kiln, number of burners, horizontal travel to the chimney, and degree of draft required by the downdraft arrangement. The cross section of the chimney should be at least equal to that of the flue. As a rule of thumb, each foot of horizontal flue must be compensated for by 2 additional feet of chimney.

Some authorities have tried to give exact figures for the dimensions of the various parts of the kiln, but since each design is something of a law unto itself, it seems best to generalize. Wherever possible, flexibility is desirable so that critical dimensions can be adjusted after the kiln is tried out. Thus, large flues can be cut down to smaller ones, bag walls can be moved or raised, and chimneys made higher if necessary.

Bernard Leach, in *A Potter's Book* ventures some rules on the proportion of kilns. In general his estimates seem far over on the generous side. For example, he recommends that the chimney diameter be $\frac{1}{4}$ to $\frac{1}{5}$ the diameter of the kiln. That would make the chimney for a 10-foot kiln at least 2 feet in diameter and a maximum of $2\frac{1}{2}$ feet, a really huge chimney. Furthermore, the height of a chimney, according to Leach, must be 25 times its diameter. Thus, for our 10-foot kiln, we would have a 50- to 75-foot chimney.[1]

[1] Bernard H. Leach, *A Potter's Book* (New York: Transatlantic Arts, 1948), pp. 190–91.

To summarize, the principle rules of kiln design are: (1) a simple rectangular or cylindrical shape, (2) ample burners or fireboxes, and room for combustion to take place, (3) good circulation, (4) adequate flue, and (5) a sufficiently large and tall chimney. Obviously, there are too many variables involved to make it possible to specify all of these aspects of the design exactly, but Figure 111 estimates the

		CRITICAL DIMENSIONS IN GAS-FIRED DOWNDRAFT KILNS		
SIZE OF KILN	NUMBER OF BURNERS	AREA OF FLUE OPENING	CROSS SECTION OF CHIMNEY	HEIGHT OF CHIMNEY
10 cubic feet	4	45 sq. in.	9″ x 9″	12 ft.
20 cubic feet	6	65 sq. in.	9″ x 9″	16 ft.
30 cubic feet	6	81 sq. in.	9″ x 9″	20 ft.
50 cubic feet	8	120 sq. in.	$13\frac{1}{2}$″ x $13\frac{1}{2}$″	20 ft.

111. *Critical dimensions of gas-fired kilns.*

sizes for flues, chimney, and the numbers of burners for various sized gas burning kilns. Many variables such as wall construction, kind of burners, and the proportions of the kiln are not taken into account, however, and such a chart should be used only as a general guide.

As indicated in the description of the historical development of the kiln, there are only a limited number of ways of circulating heat through the chamber. Each has its advantages and disadvantages. The updraft kiln is the simplest arrangement.

Figure 42 in the previous chapter on the historical development of the kiln is an example of an updraft arrangement. Three firemouths are provided at the base. The flame enters the chamber, passes up through the setting and out into the chimney at the top. It is a simple structure. The only difficulty is that the lower part of the chamber tends to fire hotter than the top.

Figure 112 shows a simple updraft arrangement for gas firing. There may be one or more burners, entering holes at the bottom of the kiln. The flame is deflected by a horizontal baffle, or floor, and passes upwards along the walls and out a flue hole at the top. By positioning the burners mostly toward the outside, an excessively hot bottom may be avoided. Small kilns of this design work quite well but tend to have cool spots either toward the top or the middle of the setting. An advantage is that, since the draft is upwards no chimney is required, and the exhaust gases can be collected in a hood. Since the escaping gases from the kiln are mixed with cool

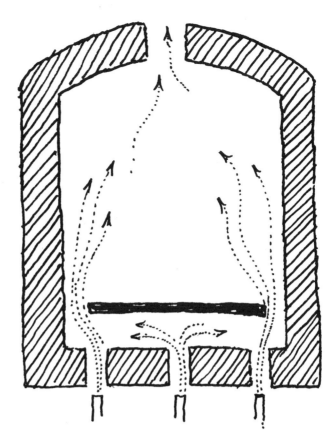

112. *Updraft circulation.*

air from the room before entering the hood, the hood can be made of metal, and may be vented through a window or simple roof vent. In such an arrangement no permanent brick chimney is required, often a considerable advantage.

A refinement of the design is shown in Figure 113. Here the burners are positioned at the sides and a baffle wall is provided. This protects the ware from direct

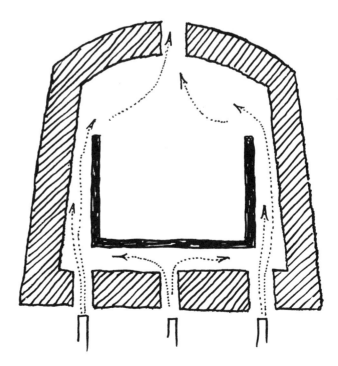

113. *Updraft circulation with partial muffle.*

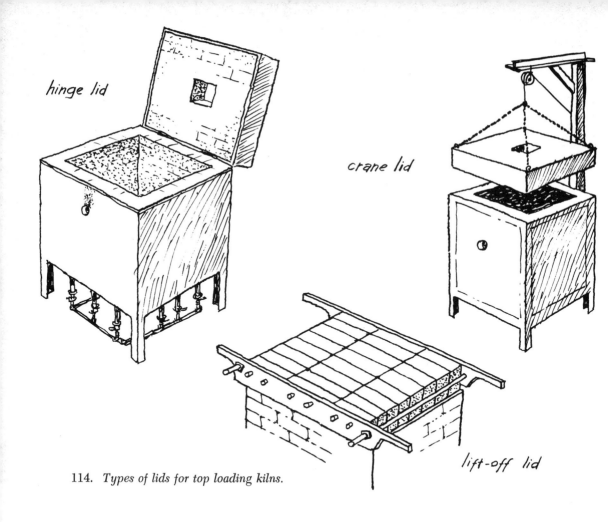

hinge lid

crane lid

lift-off lid

114. *Types of lids for top loading kilns.*

115. *A car, or shuttle kiln.*

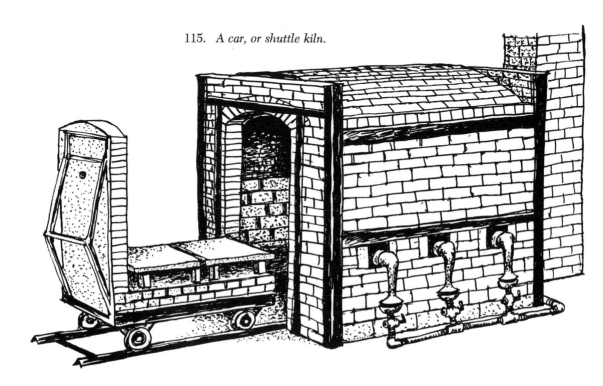

116. *Shuttle kiln manufactured by the Denver Fireclay Co.*

impingement of the flame, and if the space between the baffle and the wall is somewhat constricted at the top, more heat is released toward the top of the kiln. In this arrangement, the bottom of the kiln is apt to be cool, but this can be adjusted to some extent by letting some flame go under the baffle and enter below the setting. These updraft style kilns may be loaded through a door in the side, or through the top. Hinged lids, as shown in Figure 114, have been used, or lids moved on and off the kiln with a small mechanical lifter or crane.

In designing updraft kilns it is well to provide plenty of burners. Several small burners, while they are inconvenient to operate, help to distribute the heat. It is also well to make the flue fairly large; it can always be closed down during operation by sliding a brick or tile partially over the opening. Kilns of this type are logically heated from the bottom, rather than the sides, and the whole structure may be built up on an angle iron frame so the burners and valves may be operated below. Bunsen or Fischer burners of the type used in chemical laboratories are sometimes used for smaller kilns, and they work very well, provided there is sufficient gas pressure.

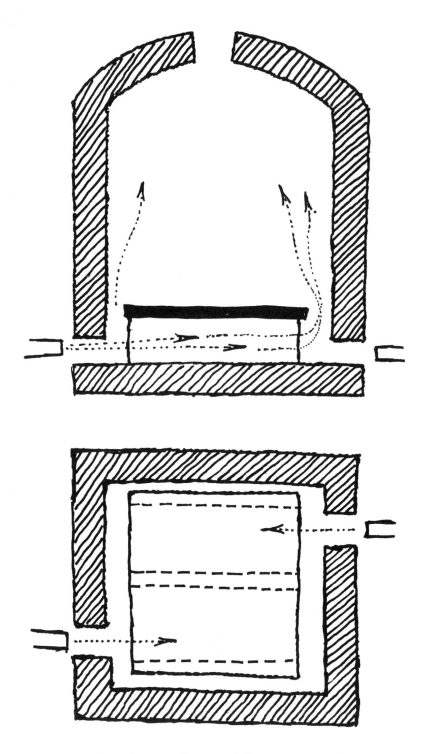

117. *Updraft circulation, with flames passing under the floor.*

118. *Dickinson updraft gas-fired kiln, manufactured by the Denver Fireclay Co.*

An updraft kiln may be no more than a squarish box of bricks with a hole in the top, a door in the front and some burners entering below. Fairly good results can be obtained in such a kiln. The difficulty of achieving perfectly even heating, however, makes the updraft kiln a less-than-perfect solution. Furthermore, if reducing conditions are desired, updraft kilns are rather unsatisfactory because of the difficulty of circulating reducing flames evenly into all parts of the setting. The path of the flame is too straight up.

Another version of the updraft kiln passes the flame under the setting. Burners are arranged at the sides, and flame goes under a floor tile, passes up along the wall and out, as shown in Figure 117. Staggering the position of four burners gives four flame channels beneath the floor. The hazard of this design is a "hot bottom," but if reducing fire is being used, the gas tends not to burn completely until it has passed under the floor tile and up on the wall, making for better heat distribution.

Updraft kilns are sometimes provided with a muffle to protect the ware from direct flame. A muffle is an inner lining or box which is set inside the kiln. The flames from the burners are directed outside the muffle, and the ware inside it is exposed neither to flame nor combustion gases. The muffle was first designed to avoid the use of saggers, which are space consuming and have a relatively short life. Many kinds of pottery need to be protected from the direct action of the fire. Included are lead-glazed wares, wares glazed in colors which are sensitive to slight reduction, and wares being fired with overglaze enamels.

Muffles present several problems of construction and operation. The muffle itself must be made of some material which conducts heat reasonably well, otherwise it would be difficult to heat the interior space. Thin plates of fireclay refractory have been used, or plates of a silimanite refractory. The best material, however, is silicon carbide. Muffles of silicon carbide are made in different sizes and designs, and are usually composed of interlocking plates for floor, walls, and arch. Complete muffles of this kind are expensive. Obviously, the kiln must be designed with the proportions of the muffle taken into consideration.

A complete muffle will have a floor, walls, and arch completely sealing off all flames, as shown in Figure 119. Partial muffles are frequently used, however, and these have been found sufficient for most types of pottery. One design for a partial muffle consists of side plates on an updraft kiln to baffle off the fire and keep it from the ware until it reaches the upper part of the kiln. When coke or peat are

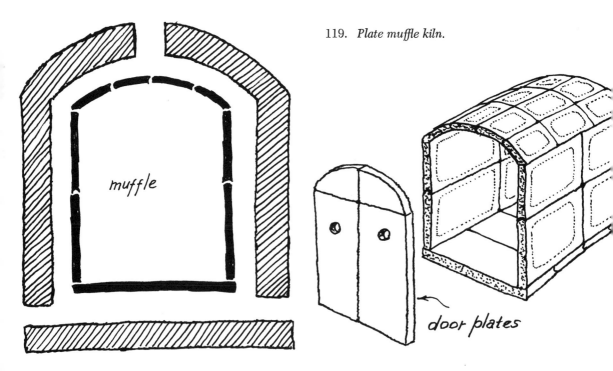

119. *Plate muffle kiln.*

muffle

door plates

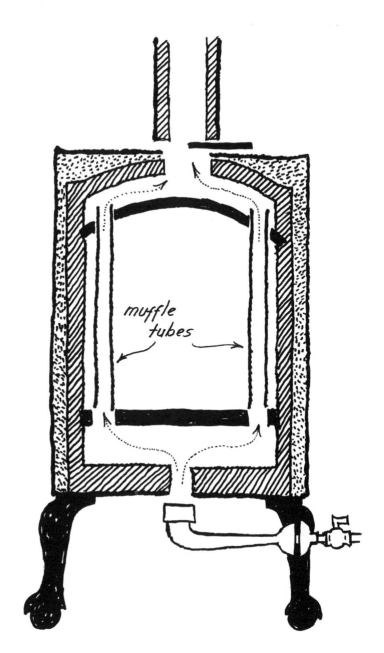

120. *Tube muffle kiln.*

used for fuel, as is sometimes done in Holland and Belgium, a muffle is built on the inside of the kiln to hold the ware, and the fuel is burned in the cavities between the muffle and the outer wall.

A tube muffle kiln is shown in Figure 120. In this system, the heat from the burners enters a lower firebox or combustion chamber, and is then led upwards through a series of refractory tubes arranged around the perimeter of the ware chamber. A collecting chamber above leads the hot exhaust gases to the chimney Portable kilns of this type, in spite of their bulk and rather high cost, formerly enjoyed considerable popularity, and they work well. Because of the large surface area of the numerous muffle tubes, heat radiation is rapid and efficient, and the

121. *Tube muffle kiln manufactured by the Denver Fireclay Co.*

ware is well protected. As with all updraft kilns, however, the bottom tends to be hot. Another disadvantage of the tube muffle kiln is the tendency of the floor of the kiln to deteriorate from continued usage. The tubes are fragile, but these can easily be replaced.

All muffles tend to impair the efficiency of the kiln because the heat must penetrate to the interior of the kiln by conduction and radiation only, without the benefit of transfer by convection to the ware, and the cost of heating a muffle kiln will be somewhat higher than an open fire kiln. Evenness of heat is a more serious problem. Without the flow of hot gases through the ware chamber there is no way of directing or altering the flow to adjust heat differences, and the owner of a muffle kiln is quite helpless to cure any unevenness that may exist. These drawbacks must be balanced off against the benefits of protection for certain kinds of glazes. But since the advent of the electric kiln, there is much less need for the muffle kiln, since electric fire performs approximately the same function, that of furnishing a clean, flame-free atmosphere. The completely muffled kiln is obviously useless for reduction firing.

The downdraft kiln might better be called the "circuitous draft kiln." As described in the section on historical development, it came about first from a cross-draft arrangement that was later modified to produce a more roundabout pathway for the flames through the interior of the kiln. This circuitous pathway serves to (a) transmit more heat from the fuel to the ware and to the inside of the chamber, therefore letting less heat escape from the chimney, and (b) enables an even distribution of heat throughout the ware chamber because the flame may be directed by baffles.

There are many different possible arrangements of burners and flues for down-draft firing, and several possibilities for the circulation of heat inside the kiln. Perhaps the best arrangement for small kilns is shown in Figure 122. Here the

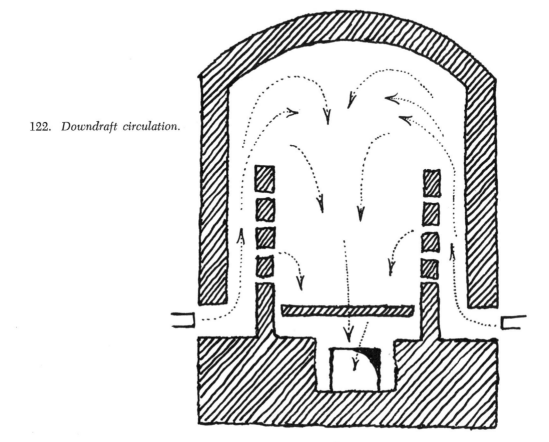

122. *Downdraft circulation.*

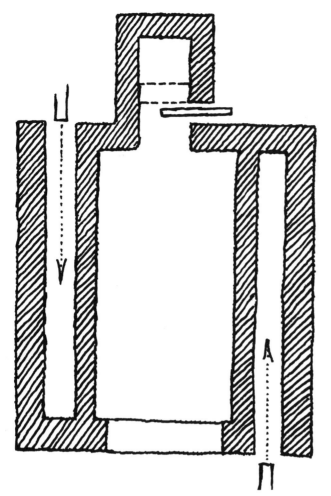

123. *Burner ports directed parallel to the bag walls.*

124. *Crossdraft circulation.*

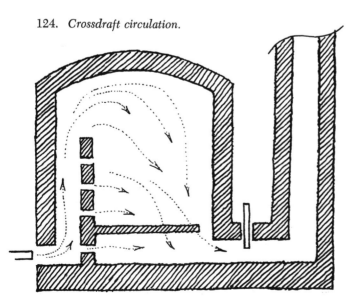

burners are arranged at the side of the kiln and the flame is deflected upwards by a baffle or "bag" wall toward the top. The flames are then pulled downward through the setting, collected in a flue at the bottom of the kiln and drawn back into the chimney, which is behind the kiln. There is really no flaw in this arrangement, and perfectly even heat distribution can be obtained in a kiln built with this type of circulation. For small oil burning kilns, the same design can be used, except that two burners are directed into the kiln the long way of the combustion spaces, as shown in Figure 123. This gives more room for combustion, a necessity for oil. One burner may enter from the front of the kiln and one from the back, or both may be mounted in the front.

In another arrangement, burners may be placed on one side of the kiln only, as shown in Figure 124. In this case, the chimney is placed on the opposite side of the kiln, and the flames pass up over a deflecting wall, down through the ware and out a flue at the bottom. It will be seen that this design is similar to one unit of an oriental chamber kiln. It has the flaw of being cold near the flue, but this can be cured, at least partially, by providing a channel that draws some of the flame directly across under the setting to the area near the flue, as in the Newcastle kilns. This arrangement is often used for wood-fired kilns where it is very desirable to have only one firemouth.

Other variations of the downdraft principle have been tried. One possibility is to place flues in the walls of the kiln. This has the advantage of yielding some additional heat from the products of combustion. But in small kilns it is difficult to collect these separate flues into an effective chimney of sufficient height. Or, the flames may be led under the setting first, as shown in Figure 128, then deflected upward and through the setting and out a flue hole near the burners. This gives very good circulation, but there is considerable stress on the floor, and there may be some difficulty in getting the top of the kiln as hot as the bottom.

All downdraft or crossdraft kilns require a chimney to furnish sufficient draft or pull to draw the gases downward or across through the setting. The hot products of combustion will only travel upwards unless induced by a draft to do otherwise. Therefore, the design and construction of the chimney is a critical factor. The chimney should, in fact, be considered an integral part of the design. Generally speaking, the flue hole into the chimney must be of generous size, and the chimney must be ample in cross section and height. Unfortunately, there is no easy formula for determining these dimensions.

In all too many cases, it is difficult or impossible to build a chimney for a proposed kiln because of the plan of the building. Existing chimneys will seldom serve, because more likely than not they are built for less severe heat conditions than kiln exhaust. If no chimney can be provided, a true downdraft kiln will be ruled out, and the choice may be narrowed to an electric kiln or an updraft gas kiln with a hood.

A valuable feature of downdraft or crossdraft circulation is the ease with which

126. *Back view of Ralph Fast's kiln. The high level of workmanship is evident.*

125. *Gas-fired kiln built by Ralph Fast at Falls Church, Va. The arrangement is crossdraft, with the burners at one side of the kiln and the flue at the other.*

127. *Stack. A burner is provided to warm the stack and induce a good draft for the early stages of firing.*

the flow of heat can be changed or redirected to secure more even temperature. If the kiln fires too hot in the lower part, this may be overcome by raising the height of the bag walls, forcing more of the flame directly toward the top of the kiln. On the other hand, if the kiln is firing too hot in the top, the reverse remedy is tried, i.e., lowering the bag walls or making larger openings in them so more of the flame will pass directly into the lower part of the setting. Adjustments can also be made to direct the flow of hot gasses either to the front or the back of the kiln. This is accomplished by changing the size and the position of the openings which lead from the ware chamber to the flue below.

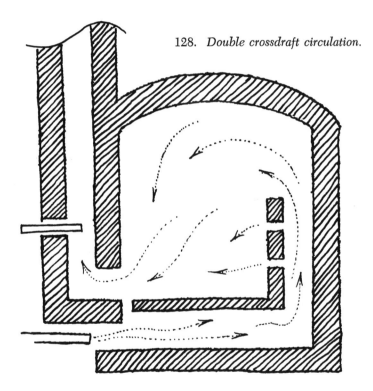

128. *Double crossdraft circulation.*

Kiln setting is discussed below, but it should be noted here that the setting vitally affects the path of flow through the kiln. If the shelves and ware are too tightly set, or if there is one area which is tightly set and another which is very open, abnormal firing may result.

Figure 129 illustrates the possibility of combining updraft and downdraft systems in the kiln. The kiln has a flue hole in the top which connects to the chimney by a lateral flue. It also has a flue at the bottom. Either one of these may be closed by a damper. Thus with the bottom damper closed, the firing will proceed updraft. A kiln of this type may be useful for firing biscuit updraft with less chance of flashing.

The idea of a double kiln is tempting, because in any kiln a great deal of heat goes up the chimney and is wasted. Another chamber can be tacked on at the back of the kiln, or the chimney can be enlarged and given a door so it will hold bisque. Before building such a double kiln, however, the ceramist should consider some of the difficulties. For one thing, the addition of a second chamber usually cuts down on the draft, and unless there is a considerable chimney, a downdraft arrangement may not work. Another trouble is the control of temperature in the second chamber. When the main ware chamber is up to glaze maturing temperature, the bisque chamber may be seriously overfired. One answer to this problem is to provide a by-pass from the first chamber to the chimney, with suitable dampers for control.

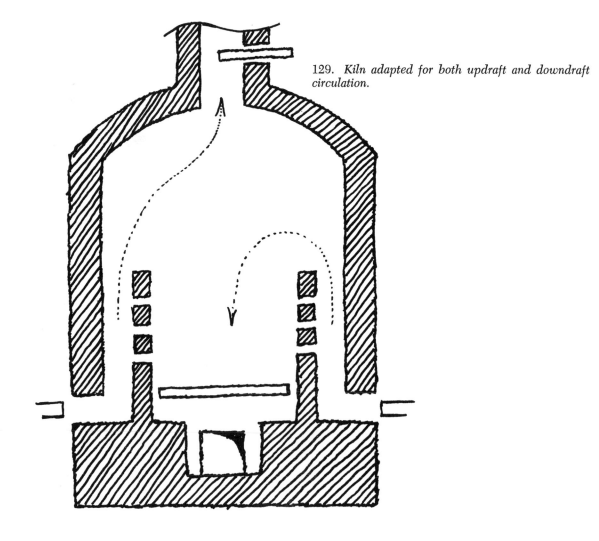

129. *Kiln adapted for both updraft and downdraft circulation.*

But this may make the structure more complex than is justified by the small savings in fuel. What is worse, shifting over to the by-pass may interrupt the temperature rise in the first chamber.

Every kiln must have a damper to adjust the pull of the chimney and to seal the kiln at the end of the firing, preventing a rush of cold air through it and up into the chimney. The damper may simply be a brick placed across the top opening in a small updraft kiln, or it may be arranged horizontally or vertically as a damper plate, as shown in Figure 131. A horizontal damper plate in the lower part of the chimney is very practical because it stays in any position. A kiln shelf may be used. A vertical or "guillotine" damper is usually made of steel and is held up by a pin through one of the holes in the plate. Metal damper plates tend to warp and to swell from the oxidizing effects of the heat, so a wide slot must be provided.

Kiln doors present no problem. On small kilns, the simplest arrangement is to brick in the door with loose bricks for each firing. Insulating bricks are usually used for this purpose. Refractory blocks to serve as kiln doors may be made from a castable refractory, or from groups of insulating brick fastened together with a mortar made of fireclay and considerable sodium silicate. Clips of ni-chrome wire are sometimes used to tie the brick together, but even when both wire and cement are used, such door blocks tend to come apart after repeated firings.

The door should not be on the side of the kiln supporting the arch, and it should be high enough so no dead pocket is formed just above the door where no ware can be set. Often, the whole front of the kiln is considered a door, or the door is without an arch or lintel buttress and is bricked up each time past the main arch. For convenience, doors are often built in steel frames hinged to the steel braces of the kiln. Or doors may be lifted vertically by counterweights in guillotine fashion, as shown in Figure 116.

When a kiln fails to perform properly, the reasons are seldom hard to find, and the difficulty can usually be corrected. If a kiln will not reach the temperature for which it was designed, the burners may be at fault. Either there are not enough burners, or the burners are not generating enough heat. To assure a normal rate of climb in temperature, there must be sufficient reserve power in the burners to more than offset the loss of heat through the walls of the kiln. Even a very poorly insulated kiln will heat rapidly if the burners are sufficiently powerful. If the burners are not generating sufficient heat, it may be that there are too few of them, or that they are not getting enough gas pressure or volume. In the case of oil, a malfunction in the system may limit the force of the burners.

Another source of failure is poor circulation through the kiln. This may be caused by the flues or the chimney being too small, or by constrictions in the flame-ways or in the setting that inhibits the flow of heat through the kiln. The symptom will be failure to achieve high temperature, or very uneven heating. The cure is to enlarge whatever constricting area is causing the difficulty.

Perhaps the most common shortcoming in ceramic kilns is uneven heating. Many

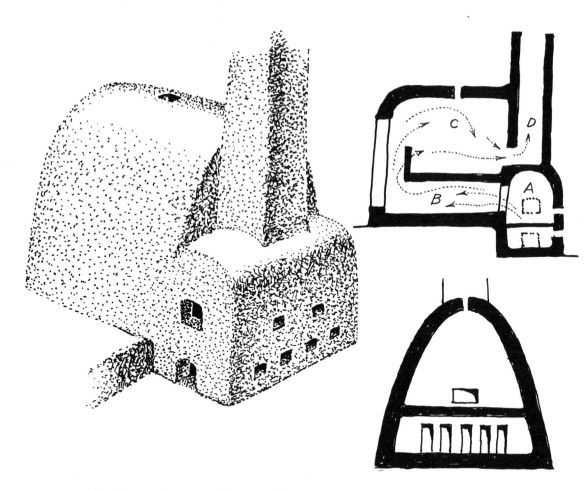

130. *Design for a wood burning kiln with double crossdraft circulation. The bottom section is used for "Bizen" effects where a lot of flashing is desired, while the upper section is relatively free of direct flame and fly ash, and can be used for regular glazed wares.*

ceramists accept this as something they have to live with, and use different glazes in various parts of the kiln to avoid having underfired ware. In updraft kilns, uneven heating is common, and there may be little that can be done about it in the way of adjustment of either kiln or setting. But in downdraft kilns the problem can usually be solved by adjustments carried out over a number of firings. A kiln which can be heated throughout with no more than one cone difference should be considered a success.

In designing a kiln, a great many factors must be taken into consideration. It is somewhat like designing a house where site, function, budget, and style will all enter into the design. Many people are hesitant to design and build a kiln for fear that much labor and expense will end in failure for unforeseen reasons and in fact there is some justification for such fears if the project is not well studied. A good starting point is the emulation of some existing kiln which operates successfully,

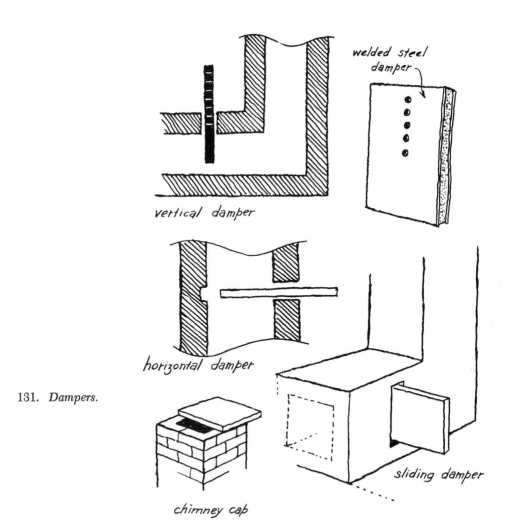

welded steel damper

vertical damper

horizontal damper

131. Dampers.

chimney cap

sliding damper

132. Doors.

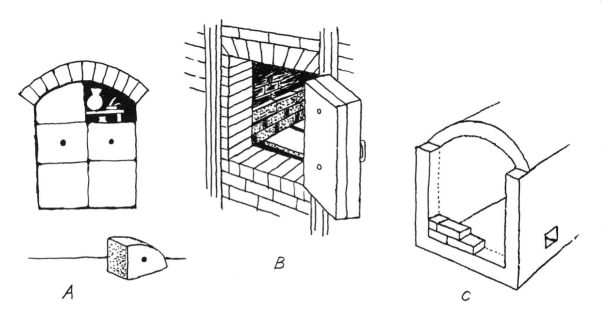

A

B

C

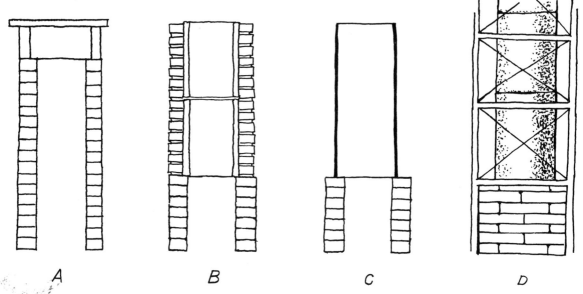

133. *Chimneys. A is a brick chimney with a cap made of a kiln shelf; B is a chimney of firebrick with the upper part made of fire-clay flue liners encased in red brick; C is a chimney with an extension of metal tubing; and D shows chimney tiles supported by metal bracing.*

and which, in type, fits the new situation. But such models may not be easy to find. It is hoped that the drawings and pictures in this book will be of help to the kiln designer, but it is almost certain that the prospective builder will have to make some changes and adaptations to suit his own particular needs. Some of the factors which will influence the design may be listed as follows:

1. Size of the space available. The kiln should be in a room which allows some work space in front, and plenty of room to walk around it to get at the burners and operate the damper. There should be ample room above and good ventilation.
2. Size of kiln desired. In general, it is good to have a kiln which is ample in size for all foreseeable needs. But if the kiln is too big, the time lapses between firings may be too great.
3. Temperature and atmosphere desired. Versatility is desirable, and if a kiln will do both high and low temperature work and will oxidize or reduce, so much the better.
4. Availability of a chimney, or the possibility of building one. If no chimney can be provided, the design choices are severely limited.
5. Availability of fuel. A decision must be made for gas, oil or bottled gas depending on the local conditions.
6. Fire regulations or zoning laws in effect at the kiln location.
7. Budget. There are some ways in which corners can be cut on expenses.
8. Kind of ware to be fired. If large and heavy sculptures are to be fired, for instance, a car kiln might be almost a necessity.
9. Permanence. If it is known that the kiln will be in use for only a short time, a different kind of structure may be indicated than if the kiln is intended to be permanent.

If all of these factors are carefully weighed, the prospective kiln builder may find that the kiln has almost designed itself. As architects often find, the program and its necessities largely dictate the shape of any new structure.

Problems of design, construction and operation become more difficult in larger kilns. Errors of construction, proportion, circulation, heat input, insulation, and draft will become greatly magnified in a large kiln of, say, 50 cubic foot capacity or more, as against smaller kilns of less than 20 cubic foot capacity.

Even when all factors involved have been carefully considered and allowed for, when the construction has been carefully done according to the best methods, and when well chosen burners and sufficient fuel are employed, it may be found that the new kiln does not perform satisfactorily. When this happens, it is well to look to variables in kiln setting and firing technique as possible causes of failure. Many a kiln has been declared a failure when in fact it could have functioned perfectly under the management of an experienced ceramist. Subtle and seemingly unimportant things such as the arrangement of the shelves, the density of setting, the control of dampers and secondary air ports, the amount of reduction and oxidation, or even the weather may drastically affect the performance of the kiln. At Alfred University we have two car kilns of identical design, placed back to back and using the same flues. In spite of the fact that these kilns are twins, they

134. *A chimney in Japan made of cylindrical tiles secured with a light steel framework. Kiln of Tokuro Kato, near Seto, Japan.*

seldom fire the same, and often it is hard to determine the factors that make one kiln fire more slowly than the other, for example, or more unevenly. If a kiln is not performing well, it is advisable to call in someone who has had experience in firing various kinds of kilns, with a view to eliminating operational mistakes first before attempting to alter the design or proportions of the kiln.

If the kiln has been built with a somewhat over-generous size of flue, chimney, combustion space and burner capacity (and all new kilns should be so built), it is quite easy to make certain adjustments to improve the firing if necessary. Flues may be diminished in size, bag walls made higher, lower, or more permeable, the path of the flames may be redirected, the chimney made taller, and as a last resort, more powerful burners may be installed. A kiln should never be written off as a failure until every remedy has been tried, and more often than not, unsatisfactory performance will be found to arise from some detail of a not too serious nature.

A new kiln should be thoroughly dried out before firing. This can be accomplished by leaving a small flame at one or more of the burners for a few hours. It is a good idea to limit the first firing to bisque temperature, allowing the new structure to settle. During this initial fire, the potter will learn a little about the temperament and individuality of the new kiln, and will have a better idea of how to manage things on the glaze fire. The first glaze fire should be stacked with pieces for which one has little hope anyway. This will mitigate the dissappointment that so frequently marks the initial firing of any new kiln. High expectations must not be indulged in. During the first firings it is wise to place numerous cone plaques throughout the kiln to determine the evenness of fire.

The kiln seems to mellow with age, and after a dozen or more firings most problems will usually disappear.

6

Electric and
Portable Kilns

THE ELECTRIC KILN is a relatively modern invention. A few electric kilns were in use in the 1920's, but it was not until the development of improved insulating refractories that the use of electricity for firing became really practical. This occurred during the thirties, and by about 1940 portable electric kilns were widely used, especially in schools. With lightweight insulating refractories, electric kilns could be made that were light in weight and thus easily portable. Moreover, kilns could be made inexpensively because of the ease of shaping the pieces of brick for various constructions and for supporting the heating elements.

The advantages of electric kilns over fuel burning kilns are obvious. The electric kiln is truly portable, being not only relatively light and compact but also requiring no chimney or vent. The kiln merely needs to be wheeled into the room and plugged in. Portability has enabled kilns to be used in thousands of situations where the installation of a fuel burning kiln would be impossible.

Not only is the electric kiln portable and adaptable for almost any space but it is easy to operate as well. No special skill or knowledge is required; to fire, one need only turn on the switches at the right time. Firings tend to be uniform, with little variation in result, certainly a great advantage for schools and for the amateur who does not want to risk firing failures. Electric kilns are also very safe to operate, because the heat is completely confined to the firing chamber. And even if, through neglect, the kiln is not turned off at the right time the worst that can happen is damage to the heating elements and over fired ware.

Since no combustion is involved, electric firing avoids the dangers involved in the burning of solid fuels. While these hazards can be reduced to a minimum by sound design and careful operation, they must be considered where the operation of the kiln is turned over to persons not trained in the work or not interested in it, as is often the case in schools. The fire itself is clean and uniform with no danger of damage to the pottery by flashing, accidental reduction or uneven atmosphere.

With such an impressive list of advantages it might be asked why the electric kiln has not completely supplanted all other types. One reason is the expense. Firing with electricity usually costs about twice as much as firing with gas or oil. This factor is perhaps not of critical importance, because firing costs per piece of pottery are very small in any case. The cost of electric power varies considerably from place to place, and in some places, such as the Scandinavian countries, electric firing is cheaper than oil and has consequently become almost universally adopted there by ceramists. Another more serious disadvantage is the size limitation. Electric kilns do not perform too well if the inside measurement exceeds $2\frac{1}{2}$ feet across. This is because the interior of the setting must be heated entirely by radiation from the elements at the walls of the kiln. Theoretically, a kiln could measure 2 feet by 2 feet across and be very tall. This would increase the capacity, but still would not permit the firing of really large pieces.

Larger electric kilns are very expensive, and the initial cost of even moderate sized ones is high considering their capacity. The cost of refractories, elements, switches, and the necessary metal case brings the total up, even for a homemade kiln. Ordnarily, a gas fired kiln can be built for less than half the cost of an electric one, and a homemade gas kiln may cost about a third as much as a similar sized factory built electric.

The life expectancy of an electric kiln is also rather low, as compared with a gas kiln. This is because the refractories are of the insulating type, and subject to wear and fatigue, especially the channels or grooves that hold the elements. The elements of the kiln give out sooner or later, necessitating repairs and expense. It is difficult to generalize about the probable life of elements, but a good Kanthal element might last for five years provided no accident in the kiln occurs. Usually elements must be replaced in a shorter time. The lower firing temperatures cause less stress on them and make for longer life.

In addition to its practical disadvantages, the electric kiln has a serious limitation in the types of ceramics which can be fired in it. Since the atmosphere in the firing chambers is constant and rather neutral, all effects involving reduction or partial reduction are ruled out. In many situations, this is not a serious limitation, but the potter who wishes to work with stoneware will never be quite satisfied with electric firing. Many potters also find the uniformity of firing in the electric kiln a hard thing to work with. They crave the accidental and often beautiful variations in color and texture which may result from the action of gas or oil flame.

The electric kiln is simple in principle. Electric current is run to resistance elements inside the kiln, and radiant heat is generated. This heat is transferred to the inside of the kiln and to the ware by radiation and conduction. The walls of the kiln are built of insulating material which impedes the transfer of heat to the outside and permits the temperature inside the kiln to approach that of the heating elements.

Electric current can be conducted through various substances. A conductor is a substance which permits the current to pass through it with relative ease, without the application of a high potential. Gases and fluids may be conductors under special conditions, but metals are the best conductors. Metals can carry a current of electricity for an indefinite period without being changed in any way except for a rise in temperature. In the atoms of silver and copper the outer electrons of the shell account for their conductivity. These "free" electrons are in the interatomic spaces and move with extremely high velocity. When an electric field is set up in the metal and current is passing through it, the velocity of the electrons increases. The drift or motion of these high speed electrons is thought to constitute the current. Collisions between the rapidly moving electrons cause the conducting metal to heat. Heat in the conductor causes an increase in electron collisions and impedes the flow of current, and for this reason even the best conductor is not perfect. Conduction can be improved by cooling; for example, if a metal such as copper or silver is cooled almost to absolute zero it will become almost a perfect conductor.

In poor conductors, the electron flow meets with resistance that may greatly slow or stop the current. A sort of electrical friction may occur, which is just the opposite of conductivity. Some non-conductors are sulphur, glass, mica, quartz, rubber, and shellac.

Means have been devised for measuring conductivity. In practice, however, it is the resistance of a substance which is measured rather than its opposite, conductivity. The unit of resistance is the *ohm*. The ohm is defined in terms of the unit of electrical potential (*volt*), and of current (*ampere*). An ohm is a resistance such that a potential of one volt causes a current of one ampere to flow through it. The resistance of a body expressed in these terms is independent of the amount of current or voltage applied, provided the temperature is constant. The resistance increases with the length of the conducting body, but diminishes with an increase in cross section. Thus a very fine copper wire will have a relatively high resistance, but a thick bar or wire will have a low resistance.

Current passing through a conductor in the form of a wire varies directly with the voltage and inversely with the resistance. This relationship is known as *Ohm's Law:* $I = \dfrac{E}{R}$ where I is amperes, E is volts and R is ohms. In other words, the intensity of current is equal to electromotive force or potential divided by resistance. By using Ohm's Law, one can determine any one of the values if the other two can be measured. The resistance of any appliance, for example can readily be determined with an ammeter and a voltmeter to measure the amperes and volts.

As an example of the application of Ohm's Law, suppose that a toaster is being designed that will draw about 10 amperes of current. What length of resistance wire will be required?

If the current is 110 volts, the equation would be:

$$R = \frac{110}{10} \text{ or 11 ohms resistance.}$$

If the wire of ribbon element being used had a resistance of 1.5 ohms/ft., it would require $\frac{11}{1.5}$ or 7.4 feet of the element.

If there were a perfect conductor, no work would have to be done to maintain a flow of electricity in it because there would be no resistance. But in practice, all conductors offer some resistance, and the energy needed to overcome this resistance is converted into heat. When electricity is to be used as a source of heat, an element is chosen which will offer enough resistance so the flow of electricity through it will generate heat. In the case of electric kilns, elements which have a high resistance must be used in order to bring the temperature up to the high temperatures needed.

For kilns to be used at modest temperatures of 1100° C. or less, elements made of alloys of nickel and chrome have been used. Elements of this type are inexpensive and give good service provided the upper limit of temperature is never exceeded. For higher firing, Kanthal elements are used. Kanthal is a patented alloy and the top rated Kanthal A-1 is serviceable at temperatures up to 1310° C. The superior performance of Kanthal elements and their usefulness at higher temperatures has made them popular for all types of electric kilns, largely displacing the ni-chrome elements. Kanthal elements are distributed by the Kanthal Corporation (Bethel, Connecticut), which furnishes a handbook giving the properties of the different available alloys. Figure 135 shows the probable life of various types of elements. The superiority of Kanthal even for low temperture work is clearly demonstrated.

All elements grow in length with use, especially ni-chrome. Kanthal grows less, and causes less trouble in bulging out of the channel provided for it in the kiln. However, Kanthal has the disadvantage of being very soft at high temperatures and very brittle when cold.

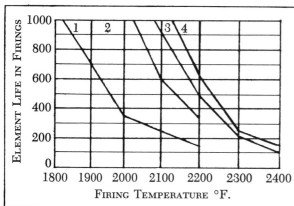

The graph at left shows the comparative number of firings that may be expected from each of four different alloys under identical conditions. Curve 1 represents a Nickel-Chromium alloy; Curve 2 represents Kanthal D; Curve 3 represents Kanthal A; and Curve 4 represents Kanthal A-1. Read vertically to compare alloys: for example, if every firing is to 2100°, A-1 will last over 1000 firings, A will last 950, D will last 600 and Nickel-Chromium only 150. Maximum temperature for equal life from each alloy may be read horizontally. Larger wire will give longer life than shown.

135. *Life expectancy of elements in electric kilns.*

The size of wire most commonly used varies from B&S gauge 14 to B&S gauge 18. The choice of wire size is optional, but the larger sizes are known to have a longer life. In practice, the larger sizes are more expensize, because larger gauge wire has less resistance and more length is needed to produce the desired heat. For elements of 1500 watts or more, wire smaller than 15 gauge should not be used. Suspended in air, a smaller gauge element reaches a higher temperature than a larger gauge element of the same wattage. Figure 136 shows the temperatures

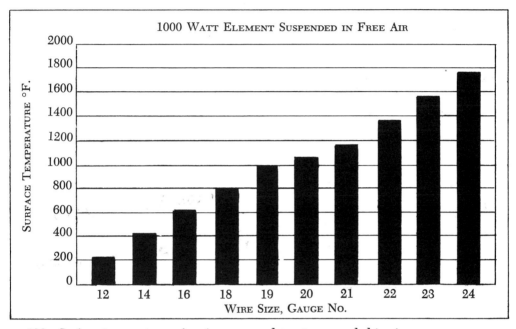

136. *Surface temperatures of various gauge elements suspended in air.*

reached, suspended in free air, by ten 1000-watt elements of different gauge. The largest wire is heated to only a little above the boiling point of water, while 24 gauge wire attains a temperature of nearly 1800° F. Each of the elements gives off the same amount of heat, but in the case of the smaller gauge wire the heat is being generated in a smaller mass and is radiated from a much smaller surface. When elements are heated in free air much of the heat is carried off by convection currents of air, and radiation is high because of the difference in temperature between the element and its surroundings. Figure 137 shows the relationship between kiln temperature and element temperature as a firing proceeds. At the beginning there is considerable difference. As heat builds up in the kiln, the temperature of the elements is raised because less heat is radiated from the element. A hotter element in turn radiates more heat, and thus the temperature of both kiln and element advances. Finally, the advance of heat in both element and kiln levels

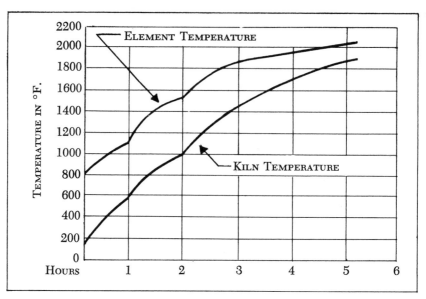

137. *Relationship between element temperatures and kiln temperature.*

off as heat loss through the walls of the kiln or the storage of heat begins to equal the amount being generated.

The amount of wattage, and thus the number of resistance and elements required to heat a given kiln requires a complex engineering calculation. There are a good many factors to be considered, such as size and shape of the kiln, the materials used for the walls of the kiln and the backup installation. But as a general rule, if stoneware temperatures are to be reached, each cubic inch of kiln space requires 1.2 watts. Thus, a kiln 18″ x 18″ x 18″ inside would contain close to 6000 cubic inches and would require 7000 watts. Five or six circuits would normally be used for a kiln of this size, since for small kilns elements of 1000 to 1500 watts have been found satisfactory. When the type of element is decided upon, and its resistance obtained from the manfacturer's data, the length of each element can be easily calculated by using Ohm's Law.

Figure 138 shows a wiring diagram for a kiln with six elements. Each element is controlled by a separate switch, and the desired advance of temperature is achieved by turning on one element at a time.[1]

The elements are coiled by wrapping the wire around a rod of suitable dimensions and installed in recesses in the kiln wall as shown in Figure 139. The recesses are cut into the soft insulating brick with an angular tool operated in a drill press. The grooves in the brick should be painted with a mixture of aluminum and kaolin to increase radiation and to lessen the reaction between the elements and the brick at high temperature. Refractory element holders are sometimes used. These have the advantage of not breaking and crumbling, but they make repairs very difficult if glaze becomes melted in them.

[1] For a detailed working drawing of an electric kiln see *Kiln Drawings and Material Lists* (State University of New York, College of Ceramics, Alfred University: Alfred, N. Y., 1965).

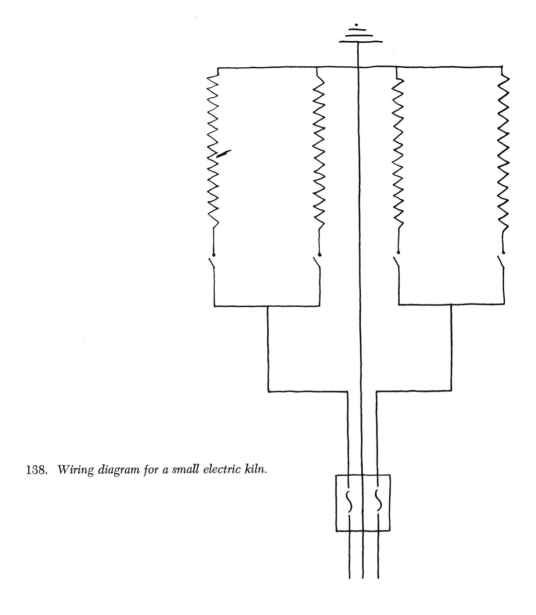

138. *Wiring diagram for a small electric kiln.*

139. *Grooves in the kiln wall for supporting the elements.*

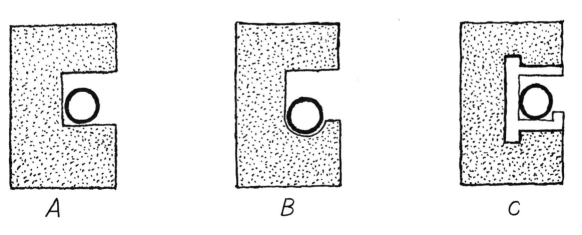

A   B   C

Figure 140 shows some different styles of electric kilns. Access may be either through a door in the front, which can be hinged and may contain heating elements, or from the top. The top loader has certain advantages; its construction is simpler and if the lid deteriorates, it can easily be repaired. A sectional kiln is another possibility. In this style, separate sections are stacked on top of each other to the desired height. Each section has its own independent element and switch.

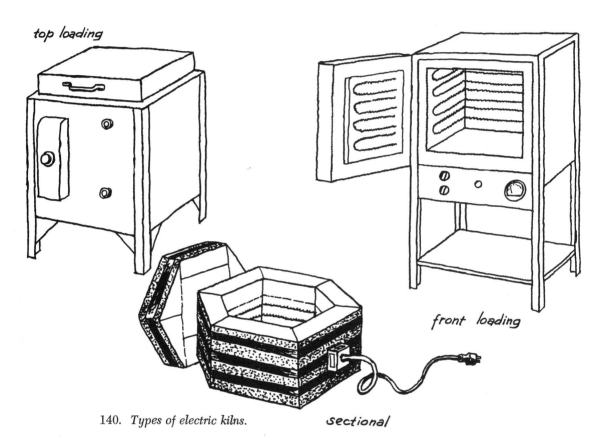

top loading

front loading

140. *Types of electric kilns.*   *sectional*

Except for the problem of supporting the elements, there are no great construction difficulties involved in building an electric kiln. K-20 refractories may be used for kilns designed for low temperature work, but better kilns are made of K-26 brick. The wall is usually made with $4\frac{1}{2}$ inches of insulating brick backed up with a thinner layer of block insulation. Solid insulation made of diatomaceous earth and asbestos fiber is the best material for backup insulation because it will not pack or settle. Front loading kilns are made with a roof formed of a low arch or jack arch, or, in the case of small kilns, with a slab roof. The exterior of the kiln is usually made in the form of a metal case. The only function of the case is to hold the kiln together for shipping, and a homemade kiln is just as satisfactory if finished with sheets of asbestos cement board held in place by a light angle iron frame.

Thicker, more highly insulating walls do not necessarily make for a more efficient kiln. If the walls are too thick, too much heat will be stored, and operation of the

141. *Washburn kiln.*

kiln will not be as economical as would be the case if the walls were thinner. Some loss by conduction through the walls and radiation from the outside is actually useful in slowing down the advance of heat toward the end of firing.

Another type of heating element used in electric kilns is known by the trade name Glo-bar. Glo-bar elements are made from carborundum in the form of rods. The rods are run through the kiln, close to the side walls, and are connected to the current on the outside. The great advantage of this type of element is that it makes higher temperatures possible, up to 1500° C. A transformer is required, however, the cost of which usually exceeds that of the kiln, and this factor of very high initial cost has in most cases prevented the use of Glo-bar kilns.

Many excellent electric kilns are on the market, and competition has brought prices into line for comparable models. Figure 141 shows a Washburn kiln, which is furnished in various sizes. It is a very well made kiln with no unnecessary external styling.[1]

There seem to be fewer incentives for building electric kilns than gas kilns, since the homemade electric kiln is in no way superior to one purchased from a manufacturer. But if the cost of one's own labor is disregarded, some savings may be made.

The first portable gas or oil fired kilns on the market were the "Revelation" and Denver tube-muffle kilns. The Denver kilns are still being made, and in spite of some obvious disadvantages they have given good service. This type of kiln requires connection to a chimney, which rules it out in some situations. To avoid the chimney problem, most portable kilns are designed to be used with a hood that collects the exhaust gases after they are sufficiently cooled to be evacuated through a window or opening on the ceiling or roof. Since this system precludes any positive draft, such kilns must be of the updraft type. Portable kilns are invariably made of insulating refractories held together in some sort of metal case. Some have front doors, usually with hinges or other devices for easy closing. Another type is top loading, with a small opening in the lid for a flue. Muffle, or semi-muffle kilns as well as open firing types are available.

Portable kilns are expensive. The initial cost is usually more than twice that of a stationary kiln of the same size, even without taking shipping costs into consideration. In spite of this greater cost, portable kilns are in no way superior to those built on the spot. They may, in fact, be decidedly inferior, in both performance and durability. But in spite of the disadvantages, there are situations where a portable kiln is the inevitable choice. These include schools or institutions which are unable to contract for building a unique appliance like a kiln, or individuals who do not feel competent to build a kiln or supervise the building of one. Or, an individual may not wish to build a kiln on rented property and therefore prefers to invest in equipment which can be moved.

---

[1] Washburn kilns are distributed by Ceramic Specialties Co., Alfred, N. Y.

PART 3

Operation of Ceramic Kilns

1

Theory of Firing

> *". . . . as for the regulation of fire, it cannot be compared with mechanical measures. For you must know that in order to make a successful batch of work, especially when it is glazed, the fire must be regulated with such careful skill that if it is not well done, you are often disappointed."*[*]
>
> Bernard Palissy   1584

From a technical point of view, the firing of ceramic objects is a very simple process, and the kiln is not complex, either in construction or operation. We have seen how heat can be generated through the combustion of fuels or by radiant electrical elements, and how such heat can be directed into a chamber and confined there to bring about elevated temperatures. The advance of temperature in the kiln is controlled by a few factors, the most important of which are the relation of input to loss, and the design of the kiln as it affects circulation and heat transfer by convection, conduction, and radiation.

The temperature of an object at any given moment is a perfectly natural attribute of matter. From a chemical point of view, heat is an indicator of the degree of molecular activity. While atoms themselves do not change with temperature, the relationship between atoms does. Higher temperatures may be thought of as an increased vibration or movement within molecular structure.

Depending on temperature, a substance may be in the solid, the liquid, or the gaseous state. An increase in temperature loosens the molecular bonds between atoms and permits the increased flow and mobility noted in liquids and gases compared to solids. There is no such thing as a "normal" temperature. This is a concept which we have gained by our experience as organic living beings, and hence our need for an ambience restricted to a certain temperature range in order to survive.

---

[*] *Op. cit.*

But water is just as "comfortable" in the form of ice or water vapor as it is as the more familiar liquid. Chemically, all three forms are the same substance, but the physical state varies according to the temperature. If the world were limited to temperatures in excess of 100° C., water and ice would be as foreign to it as volatilized silica, for instance, is to our environment.[1]

When we raise the temperature in a kiln, the material inside should not be thought of as being under some sort of stress, subjected to a sort of Hades. Firebricks, for all we know, may "feel" better at 1350° C. than they do at 30° C.

But in one sense, high temperatures could be regarded as "abnormal." Heated bodies will transfer their heat to cooler bodies, and in nature the operation of this law means that concentrations of heat, whether on the earth or in the solar system or outer space will be dissipated or transferred to cooler matter by conduction or radiation. If the energy (and heat) producing reactions of substances is regarded as finite, then the entire universe must be thought of as running down, and approaching, however slowly, absolute zero, a kind of molecular death.

To achieve elevated temperatures within the kiln, it is necessary to put in more heat than is being lost. We have discussed the generation of heat by various fuel burners, and the transfer of this heat by convection and radiation to the inside of the kiln. Some of the heat so transferred escapes through the flue and some through the walls, floor, and roof of the kiln. Since gases must pass through the kiln to bring in the heat, some heat is inevitably lost through the flue. And since no insulating material, even a vacuum, is a perfect heat barrier, some heat is bound to be lost in and through the walls.

Actually, a periodic kiln, from an engineering point of view, must be regarded as a very inefficient machine because so little of the heat energy expended is used in heating the ware itself; the greater part of the heat goes into heating the kiln, or out the flue. According to Norton,[2] the heat balance in the most efficient kiln is as follows:

Useful heat applied to the ware	20%
Heat lost in cooling	18%
Heat lost through the flue	36%
Heat lost through walls and crown	18%
Heat stored in walls and crown	14%
Heat used in vaporizing moisture	8%
Incomplete combustion of fuel	6%

An increase in temperature is dependent on the input capacity of the burners; they must generate and transmit to the kiln more heat than is being stored or lost.

[1] See Norton, F. H., *Refractories* (New York: McGraw-Hill, 1949), Chapter IV, for an excellent brief account of some fundamental concepts of matter.

[2] F. H. Norton: *Elements of Ceramics*, (Cambridge, Mass.: Addison-Wesley, 1952), p. 138.

A general principle of kiln construction is that there needs to be plenty of reserve power in the burners to overcome heat losses and to elevate the temperature at a satisfactory rate. If the burners are weak (or if the kiln is lacking in insulation), the gain of heat will be too slow or nonexistent. For flexibility in firing schedules it is useful to be able to heat the kiln rapidly, although it may not always be desirable to do so.

The process of firing ceramics ordinarily involves gradually heating the kiln up to the degree needed to do the desired work on the ware, then cooling it, again gradually, to room temperature. Seldom is any prolonged holding at one temperature necessary, as in the case of cake baking. Cooling is usually accomplished by shutting off the fires and allowing the heat to escape naturally through the walls and flue. A proper firing cycle, or schedule of advancing and receeding temperature, is determined by the nature of the materials being fired and the changes desired in them. For a discussion of the heat treatment of clays and glazes, the reader is referred to this author's *Clay and Glazes for the Potter*.[1]

Ordinarily, ceramics require a rather slow heating schedule. Time is required for the various reactions to occur which change raw clay and unfused glaze materials into the finished, fired piece. Slow cooling is also necessary to prevent damage to the ware from shock and sudden contraction. The kiln must also be heated so that the temperature advances steadily, without any erratic gains and losses. These irregularities in heating can be damaging to glazes and may cause pyrometric cones to give an inaccurate indication of the end point of the firing.

Not only should the kiln heat up and cool down evenly and to the desired degree of temperature; it should also heat up evenly in all parts of the ware chamber. Many kilns that are satisfactory in every other way fire unevenly. Almost all kilns fire with a difference of at least one-half cone from one part of the kiln to another, but this difference is easily tolerated. Much ingenuity in kiln design and construction has been directed toward the ideal of an even fire.

The ideal kiln is also one in which the atmosphere can be controlled from oxidation to reduction. Many kilns that fire with gas or oil work well in reduction but will not fire oxidized ware, such as lead-glazed pottery, without flashing and partial reduction. Such kilns are as limited in their way as the electric kiln which can produce only oxidized ware.

[1] Daniel Rhodes, *Clay and Glazes for the Potter* (Philadelphia: Chilton Book Co., 1957).

2

Kiln Setting and
Kiln Furniture

"As for the right method of filling the kiln, it requires a special geometry."
Bernard Palissy[1]

In the old days, most firing was accomplished without benefit of props or shelves in the kilns. Kiln furniture is a relatively modern invention. If pottery is unglazed, and if the firing falls short of vitrifying the ware, making it subject to warping and deformation, pieces can be piled up in the kiln rather haphazardly. In the primitive bonfire style of firing, the pottery is just piled together in a closely packed mass without much regard for how the pieces fit together.

With the advent of glaze, however, an arrangement had to be devised to keep the pots from sticking together. This has been done in various ways. One way is to stack the pots one on another, but have them touch only at points which are unglazed, or to separate the pots with small wads of clay which leave only a small scar in the finished glaze. Figure 142 illustrates how this is accomplished. Bowls may be stacked one on another, with the foot of the bowl resting on an unglazed circle of the bowl below. Or bowls may be set in a column, rim to rim and foot to foot. Smaller pieces may be put inside larger ones, and lids of jars or teapots may support pieces above to form stacks of similar shapes. It will be seen that where there is variety in production, different shapes can be set with great ingenuity so that the kiln is packed closely. Stacks of pots must be somewhat limited in height because of the possibility of the bottom pieces breaking under pressure from above. Earthenware plates are sometimes stacked on their rims and leaned against each other with small clay wads between, but this arrangement can be done only if the

[1] *Op. cit.*

clay body is in no danger of warping from the fire, as in the case of very soft earthenware.

In the ancient kilns of Japan the pots were set directly on the earthen floor. To accommodate the pots to the sharply sloping angle of the floor a wedge-shaped pad of clay was placed under the pot. The degree of slope in the kiln can be reconstructed from an examination of surviving pads, even when no other trace of the kiln remains. Some old Japanese pots have a glaze that runs down the wall in a diagonal direction, a sure sign that they were fired on a slant.

The sagger is a protective box made of clay, which holds the ware in the kiln. Its purpose is to support the pottery, making it possible to fill the kiln to any height, and to protect the ware from direct contact with the flame and hot gases from the fire. In the case of kilns fired with wood or coal, saggers are practically a necessity if uniformly glazed and colored ware is desired. Ware fired in the open atmosphere of the wood or coal fired kiln will be subject to flashing, discoloration and unfore-

142. *Methods of setting various pottery forms in the kiln.*

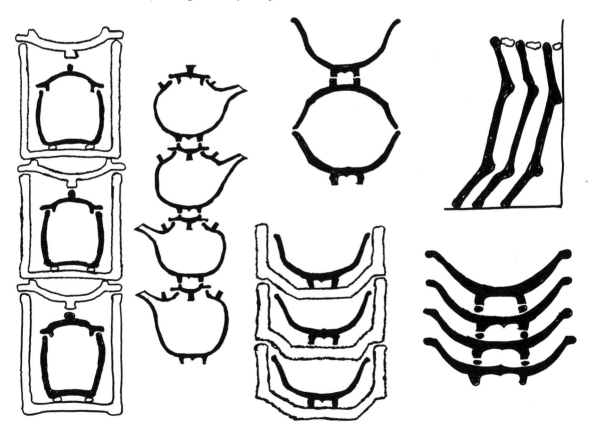

143. *Water jugs stacked in Spanish kiln. Photo by Tony Prieto.*

144. Saggers.

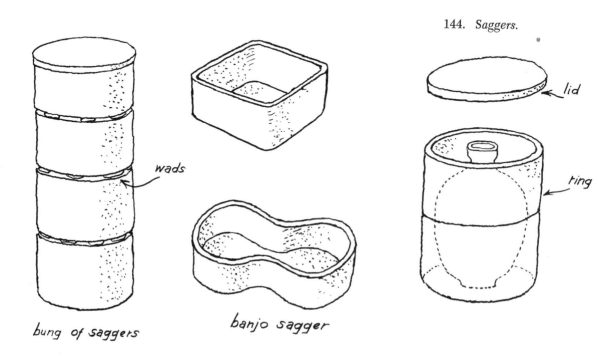

lid

wads

ring

bung of saggers

banjo sagger

145. *Unstacking a Japanese kiln. The small jars have been fired inside the larger flowerpots which serve as saggers.*

seen deposits of glaze or partial glaze from the action of ash. While these accidents might be courted by the art potter, they are not welcomed in industrial production. Saggers are especially important in the coal-fired kiln because if sulphurous fumes come into direct contact with melting glazes, they may cause bubbling or pitting.

Figure 144 illustrates various kinds of saggers. The sagger may be round, oblong, square, or "banjo" shaped depending on the shape of the ware. Rings without bottoms are used to extend the height for taller pieces. The saggers are stacked on each other in the kiln, with wadding in between for a good bearing and to seal the inside from the kiln atmosphere. Old Chinese pottery was often fired with a sagger provided for each piece, like the bowl with its individual box shown in Figure 142. These saggers could be stacked together to form tall columns or bungs.

Saggers are made of plastic fireclays, preferably those with a good resistance to thermal shock. In the old days saggers were made by hand, and each pottery of any size had a sagger shop. Now they are usually produced by pressing or casting. Saggers have a relatively short life, often no more than about 25 to 30 firings, and therefore represent a considerable expense for the potter. To keep crumbs of clay from shedding, the inside of the sagger is frequently covered with a wash of some vitrifying combination of clay, flint, and flux.

Saggers consume a great deal of space in the kiln, and if the potter tries to set a small kiln using saggers he may be able to get only a few glazed pieces in. One reason for the relatively huge kilns in the Orient was the use of saggers to support the ware.

The use of saggers is declining. With the advent of gas and oil, a cleaner oxidizing fire became possible, eliminating the need for saggers for many types of ceramics. For lead-glazed pottery and for overglaze enamels, electric kilns and muffle kilns are generally used. The studio potter who uses reduction firing obviously has no need of saggers, for he seeks the very effects which saggers were designed to prevent. The average pottery student today may never have heard of a sagger, and probably has never seen one.

Shelves and posts are the most efficient furniture for setting the kiln. With them the space can be packed like a kitchen cupboard. Shelves may be of fireclay. Clay shelves are inexpensive, but their strength is not great, so they must be made quite thick to avoid breakage. A clay tile 12" x 24" must be at least 1½" thick, and preferably thicker. Such shelves are heavy and awkward to handle.

The potter with a bent toward self-sufficiency can make his own shelves. A mixture of half fireclay and half well sized grog, mixed to a stiff plastic consistency, is pounded into a wooden mold with a mallet. Dense packing is important. The green shelves should be bedded in sand or grog and fired to at least cone 11, preferably higher. While shelves are hard to make, and not wholly satisfactory, good posts can be easily made by rolling out the fireclay into heavy snakes and cutting to the desired length. A thickening at both ends gives the post better stability. Nine-inch firebrick soaps make excellent posts, and if a brick saw is available, the soaps and splits can be cut into segments for shorter lengths.

Factory made shelves are of two general types. One is made from high-alumina materials such as silimanite, kyanite or aluminum oxide bonded with clay. Such shelves are highly refractory and give satisfactory service, especially in smaller sizes. But the ideal material for shelves is silicon carbide. Silicon carbide is made by fusing coke and sand. Electric arc furnaces are used, and a very high temperature is required for the reaction. The fused material is ground, sized, bonded with clay, pressed into the desired shapes and fired to form a hard, dense body. Silicon carbide is highly refractory and has excellent hot-load strength. Its thermal conductivity is approximately 10 times that of firebrick, which makes it an ideal material for muffles. This high conductivity also favors even heating in the case of kilns set with numerous shelves. Silicon carbide shelves are rather brittle and must be handled with care. Slow heating and cooling will greatly prolong the life of kiln shelves. The shock of rapid cooling, especially at or about red heat, causes early failure. In most cases the high initial cost of silicon carbide shelves is justified by their long life.

Kiln shelves are commonly given a coating of kiln wash. This prevents any glaze that might drip onto the shelf from sticking permanently. A good kiln wash is a

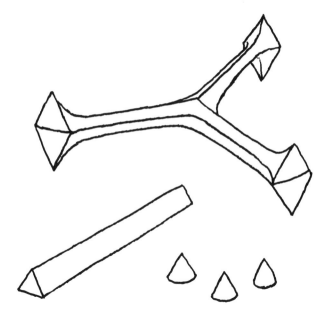

146. *Spur, pin, and points.*

mixture of equal parts of flint and kaolin, mixed with water to the consistency of thick paint. New shelves may be given two coats of wash, just enough to cover them thoroughly. Any glaze which drips onto the shelf can be loosened with the chisel or brick set. Frequent renewal of the kiln wash is advisable, but care must be taken not to let too much wash accumulate on the shelf. An occasional scraping of the shelf and cleaning with a wire brush will prevent heavy deposits of wash from making the surface rough and uneven. Kiln wash is applied only to the upper surface of the shelf.

In addition to saggers, shelves and props, other aids to kiln setting have been developed. Figure 146 illustrates spurs, pins, and points which are used to hold the ware up off the shelf, thus preventing the glaze on the bottom of the pieces from sticking. Spurs touch the glazed surface only with a sharp point, leaving a hardly

147. *Tile setters.*

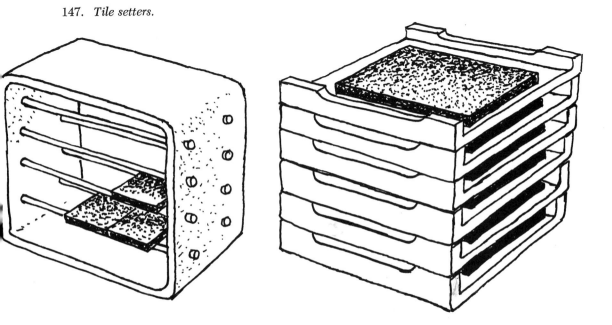

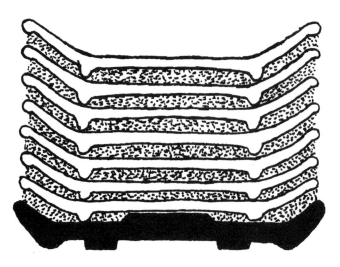

148. *China plates stacked for bisque fire.*

noticeable scar in the glazed surface which is easily ground off. The small points can be made from kaolin and fired in a glaze kiln prior to use. These props are made for pieces which are to be glazed on the bottom. They are unnecessary when the foot of the piece is clean of glaze.

Tiles are usually set in special tile furniture as shown in Figure 147. Each setter may be used for one large tile or for several small ones. They are stacked on top of each other. Another type of tile setter uses refractory rods supported in a frame, with the tiles placed on the rods for firing.

In the manufacture of china, special supports are necessary for the bisque firing, which is done at high temperature to vitrify the clay body. Since the pieces become soft at the height of the fire, they must be supported to prevent warping, slumping or distortion. This is especially true of plates, saucers, and other flat shapes. Plates may be fired in a stack, as shown in Figure 148. The bottom plate is supported on a refractory setter, shaped to receive the form of the bottom of the plate. The spaces between the plates are packed with sand or with a mixture of sand and kaolin. This packing, which must be carefully done to insure even density, holds the plates in shape during the fire. Thin china plates may be fired upside down on cranks, as shown in Figure 149. Each plate has its own support, and the cranks are designed

149. *Cranks for holding china in the bisque fire.*

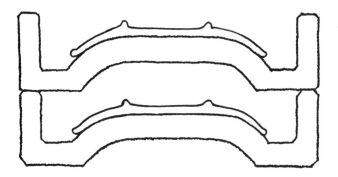

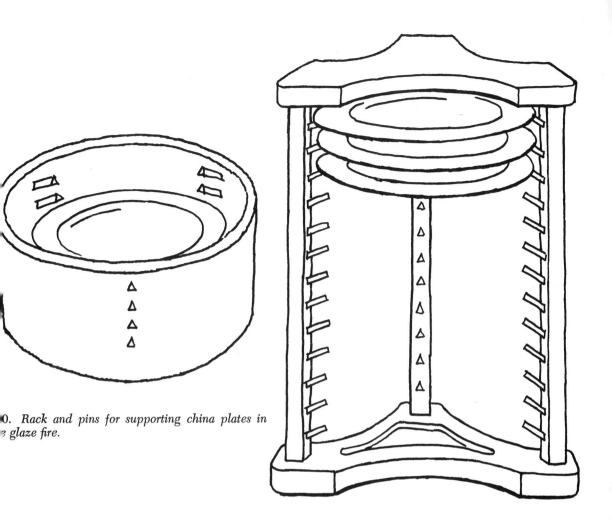

150. *Rack and pins for supporting china plates in the glaze fire.*

to stack one on the other with the plates in between. The curve of the crank, which is made of a refractory material, is designed to allow the plate to shrink upwards during the fire. These setters take up a great deal of space in the kiln and are used only for expensive china. In china manufacture, hollow ware such as teapots, pitchers, and covered bowls require no special furniture, because the form of such pieces makes them self-supporting, even when the clay body softens in the fire.

China plates are supported in the glaze fire on racks and pins or in saggers with pin supports, as shown in Figure 150. Since the glaze fire is considerably lower in temperature than the vitrifying bisque fire, there is no danger of the plates warping, and they can be supported from only three points. The pins make a slight scar in the glaze on the back of the plate, but this is ground off and becomes hardly noticeable.

Pottery manufacturers have developed varieties of kiln supports and furniture for many special shapes and to fit the particular needs of their production. Such special supports, designed for specific items of manufacture, are obviously feasible only for mass production. The studio potter who makes one-of-a-kind pieces will usually need only shelves and props.

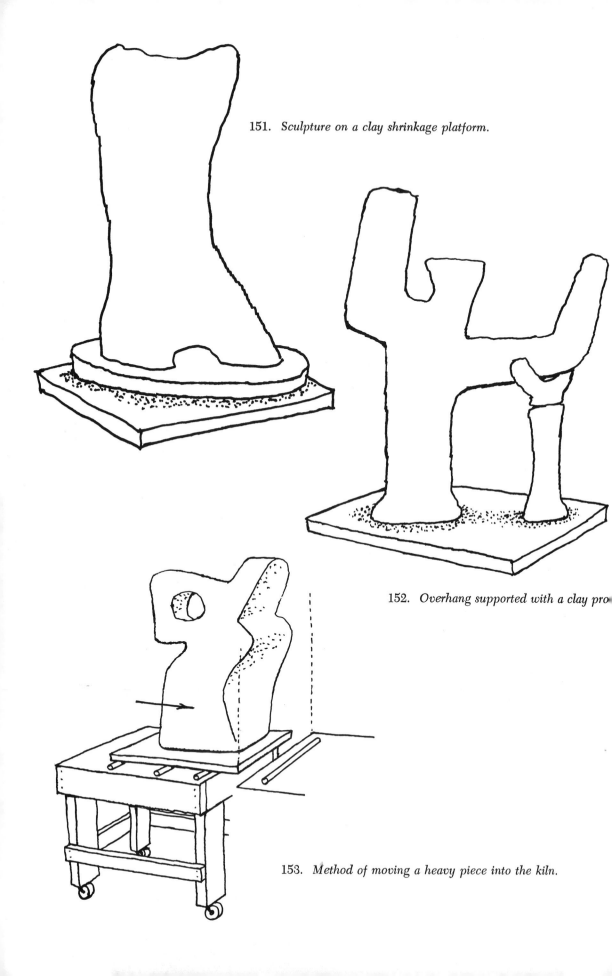

151. *Sculpture on a clay shrinkage platform.*

152. *Overhang supported with a clay pro*

153. *Method of moving a heavy piece into the kiln.*

Large ceramic pieces, such as sculpture or very large pottery forms, may require special treatment in setting and firing. Figure 151 shows a shrinkage platform, which allows the piece to shrink during the fire without cracking. Grog is spread on the kiln shelf and on this is placed a slab of clay of the same composition as the piece to be fired. The piece is placed on the slab, again with grog used as a lubrication between them. During the fire, both slab and piece shrink inwards.

Some forms may require props to keep them in shape during the fire. Figure 152 shows a form with extreme overhangs which are supported by posts of the same

154. *Temporary kiln built by Ronald Brown in Iowa City to fire a large sculpture. The kiln, built of insulating firebrick, is adapted to the shape of the piece, and burner ports are provided as needed. After firing, the kiln is dismantled. Photo by Ronald Brown.*

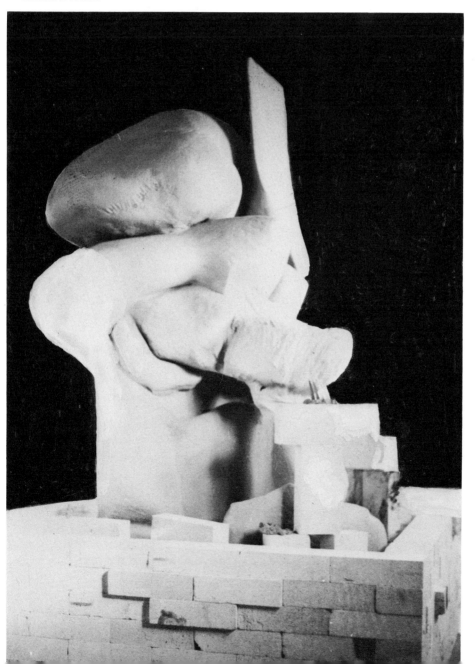

clay as the object. Such posts may be quickly made as hollow cylinders on the potter's wheel. They are put in place when both the piece and props are bone dry. It will be seen that by using sufficient props in the right places, a form of almost any shape or complexity can be fired without slumping. The piece and its props shrink together, making for continuous support during the firing. The props are discarded afterwards.

Moving large, heavy pieces into the kiln presents a problem. In a system which I worked out for my sculptures, a kiln shelf with a large piece on it is moved into the kiln on rollers, as shown in Figure 153. The rollers are $\frac{1}{2}$-inch dowel sticks. If the sculpture is made on a table the same height as the floor of the kiln, the piece is easily rolled from the table to the kiln. The table is provided with casters so it can be wheeled right up to the kiln door. The dowels, which are under the kiln shelf,

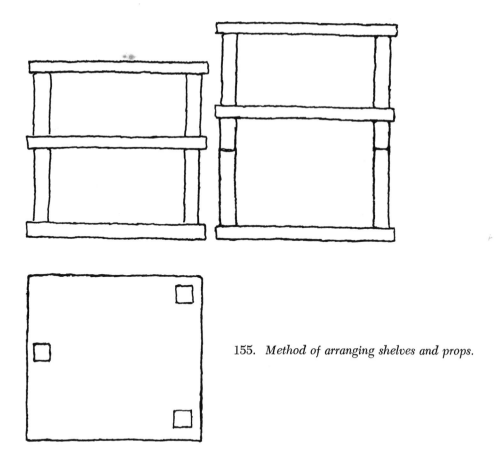

155. *Method of arranging shelves and props.*

may be left there to burn out during the fire. Another method of moving large pieces is to place them on greased panels of masonite, which permit easy sliding from one place to another. The masonite panel is left there to burn out. Large pieces may also be built on plywood and moved into the kiln, where the plywood burns away during the firing.

In fuel burning kilns the arrangement of shelves, ware and posts must be open enough and loose enough to permit the circulation of heat. If there are two sets of shelves, it is a good idea to stagger their height, as shown in Figure 155. This permits more circulation between the shelves. The kiln setting should be solidly built up, with all shelves well supported and all posts reasonably vertical. All kiln shelves should be supported on only three posts, lined up one over the other. Wads of fireclay are often used to secure a firm structure of shelves and posts. The experienced potter learns to utilize every cubic inch of available space and it is always a source of wonder how many pots can be packed into a given space. Provided circulation space is allowed, kilns generally fire much better when fully packed with pots.

3

Oxidation and Reduction

In FUEL BURNING KILNS the atmosphere can be easily controlled. Various atmospheres have an important effect on glaze and body colors and textures. (For information on reduction effects, see *Clay and Glazes for the Potter* by the author.[1])

In oxidizing fire, plenty of air is let into the burners to oxidize or burn the fuel thoroughly. This air, which enters the burners and mixes with the gas before combustion, is called primary air. Air that enters through the burner ports, not through the burner itself, and adds oxygen to the flame is called secondary air. It is pulled or sucked into the the kiln by the pull of the draft. The sign of a clear or oxidizing fire is a clear atmosphere in the kiln, everything being sharply visible. There will be a total lack of visible flame at the damper or coming from the spy holes. The flame at the burners should be burning with a predominantly blue color, with little yellow flame appearing.

If too much air enters the kiln from the secondary air accesses, there may be a cooling effect that prevents the kiln from gaining temperature. Only enough air for proper combustion should be allowed to enter. Even in the case of the air which supplies oxygen for combustion, the fraction of nitrogen must be warmed and passed through the kiln.

If the kiln appears to be oxidizing, yet no temperature gain is noted, it is probable that too much air is being admitted.

Perfect oxidation is hardly attainable in ceramic kilns. An analysis of the flue gases will always reveal the presence of some carbon dioxide. But for all practical purposes, if the kiln is burning clear without flame or smoke, an oxidizing effect will be achieved.

[1] *Op. cit.*

COLOR SCALE FOR TEMPERATURES		
COLOR	DEGREES CENTIGRADE	APPROX. CONE RANGE
Lowest visible red	475°	None
Lowest visible red to dark red	475–650	022–019
Dark red to cherry red	650–750	018–016
Cherry red to bright cherry red	750–815	015–014
Bright cherry red to orange	815–900	013–010
Orange to yellow	900–1090	09–03
Yellow to light yellow	1090–1315	02–12
Light yellow to white	1315–1540	13–20
White to dazzling white	1540 and higher	20 and above

156. *Color scale for temperature.*

If the kiln is oxidizing, a satisfactory rate of climb usually results. To advance the temperature, either the valves are turned up from time to time, or additional burners started. The damper is ordinarily left open, but if the kiln is pulling in too much air, the damper may be partially closed to diminish the draft. To advance the heat, it is good to follow some sort of schedule, for a regular pattern of temperature climb. The operation simply involves feeding sufficient fuel in through the burners to maintain the desired rate of climb. Beginning at about cone 1, carbon in the wares (and there is always some) burns, and there is an endothermic reaction that may cause a rise in temperature not attributable to the burner settings. Also at about this heat, radiation from one surface to another seems to make for a more rapid climb.

To reduce, the air supply is cut back. Either the primary air or the secondary air supply may be diminished, or both may be cut back until the flames begin to burn with a yellow color. The damper should be closed somewhat until a back pressure develops in the kiln. This will be evidenced by some flame at the spy hole. Flame will also be observed at the damper.

Extremely heavy reduction does no good. It is quite unnecessary to have great belching clouds of black smoke coming from the spy holes and chinks in the kiln. The eternal questions are when to reduce, and how much to reduce. As a general rule a neutral to light reduction gives a good color and texture. It will be necessary, however, to experiment with a new kiln to determine just what the symptoms of sufficient reduction are. Once a satisfactory firing pattern is arrived at, it can be repeated successfully.

Since reduction involves an excess of unburned carbon in the firing chamber, too much reduction is a waste of fuel. Heavy reduction will usually halt the advance of temperature, or even cause a loss of temperature. If the temperature in the kiln is not advancing, admitting more air at the primary or secondary sources of air will sometimes bring about satisfactory rate of climb.

Reduction in the earlier stages of firing, from about 750° to 900° C., will cause a deposit of some carbon in the clay being fired, the so-called "body reduction." This may produce warm browns or orange color in stoneware clays. Too much reduction at this stage, however, may cause bloating or cracking, especially if the later stage of the firing is rapid.

Heavier reduction toward the end of the firing tends to slow the kiln down and give some "soaking", usually beneficial. At this stage, reduction may also favor the development of celedon and copper red glaze colors.

Kilns always tend to re-oxidize on cooling, because they are not really airtight enough to keep oxygen out. Clay colors are developed toward warm brown by the

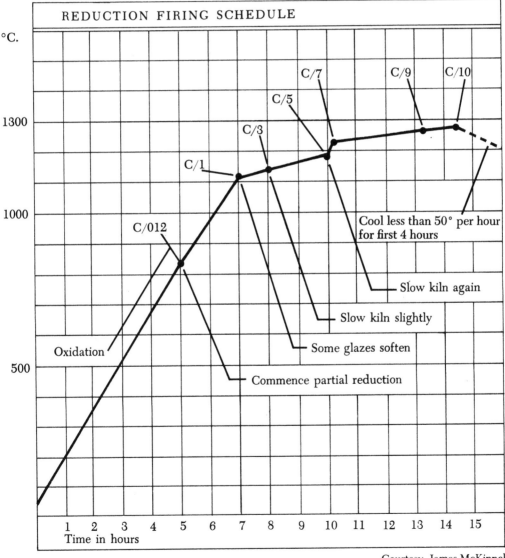

Courtesy, James McKinnel

157. *Reduction firing schedule.*

effect of this re-oxidation on the iron of the body. Some potters give the kiln a brief period of sharply oxidizing fire at the end to "clean it up," but it is rather doubtful that this has any real effect.

For reduction firing, best results are obtained in a downdraft kiln that circulates gases to every part of the setting. Figure 157 is a typical reduction firing schedule. Kilns burning wood can be reduced by adding an excess of fuel. To maintain temperature advance, and to bring about a pattern of intermittent reduction, this overstoking must be alternated with lighter stoking. Reduction firing may be damaging to the firebrick of the kiln, especially if the brick contains considerable iron. The iron may catalyze the deposition of carbon within the pores of the brick, causing a tendency to disintegrate. In practice this is nothing to worry about because in all ordinary reduction firings there is ample opportunity for the carbon to burn during the long cooling period under oxidizing conditions.

4

Temperature Measurement and Control

THE COLOR OF the inside of the kiln gives a good indication of its temperature, varying from a dull cherry red as the color first appears to almost white heat as it reaches high fire.

With experience, the kiln fireman usually knows when to shut off the fires. More exact temperature indicators are available, however. The draw trial has been widely used. Small trials are set up at the spy hole, sometimes shaped like rings. As the firing nears completion, the potter hooks out the test with an iron rod, cools it in water, and examines it to tell if the firing has melted the glaze sufficiently. Several trials may be drawn out at intervals. Because of the quick cooling, the color of draw trials usually is not indicative of what the glazed ware will be like, but the fusion of the glaze is precisely revealed. Draw trials indicate the actual change in the pottery being fired, but do not of course, indicate temperature.

Josiah Wedgwood worked out an ingenious refinement of the draw trial. This was a small disk made of clay, which of course shrank as the firing proceeded. When the disk was taken from the kiln and cooled, it was placed in a measuring device. The amount of shrinkage was an indication of the progress of the firing. In some brick kilns today, the finish of the firing is gauged by measuring the shrinkage of the mass of brick in the kiln.

The most widely used device for measuring the temperature in kilns is the pyrometric cone. A cone is a small pyramid made of ceramic material which will melt and bend at a certain degree of temperature and can be observed inside the kiln through a spy hole. The pyrometric cone was invented by the noted German ceramist Herman Seger and first described in a paper written by him in 1886. At that time the exact measurement of the higher temperatures was impossible,

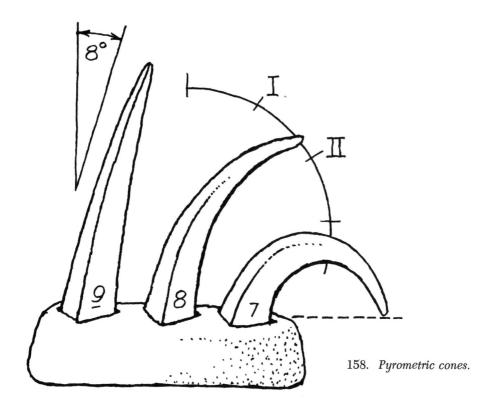

158. *Pyrometric cones.*

because the thermocouple, although known, had not been adapted to withstand red heat or more. Ceramists knew that different ceramic compositions had different melting points, as in the case of glazes, but no one before Seger had hit upon the idea of using the melting of ceramic materials themselves as a temperature indicator. He experimented with different mixtures and with the proper shape for the cone. He called the cones "*kegel*" or "'bowling pins." This has been translated as "cone," even though the shape is a truncated trigonal pyramid.

Seger did not calibrate his cones with temperature, and indeed he had no means of doing so. But he sought for a series of compositions that would fuse at regular intervals in the scale of temperature. He started with what is now known as cone 4, which he formulated by finding the lowest melting composition of clay, potash feldspar, and lime. He called this "cone four" because the molecular formula contained 4.00 mols of SiO_2.[1] He then worked on the series from cone 4 upwards. At a later time, the lower series was worked out, and the numbers below 1 were assigned a zero in front, which accounts for the somewhat confusing numbering system for the cones. The series now goes from cone 022, which is just above red heat, to cone 42, which fuses at 2015° C. Cone 42 is made of pure aluminum oxide, while cone 022 is a lead-borosilicate compound. The large sized cones are 2½″ long, and the small size are 1⅛″ long. The larger cones bend about 25° lower than the small series. The small cones are used where space in the kiln is limited.

[1] The empirical formula for cone 4 is: $\begin{array}{c|c|c} K_2O \cdot 3 & Al_2O_3 & SiO_2 \\ CaO \cdot 7 & \cdot 35 & 4 \cdot 00 \end{array}$. This composition makes a satisfactory cone 11 glaze.

END POINTS OF PYROMETRIC CONES WHEN HEATED AT 20° CENTIGRADE PER HOUR			
CONE NUMBER	END POINT	CONE NUMBER	END POINT
012	840° C.	1	1125
011	875	2	1135
010	890	3	1145
09	930	4	1165
08	945	5	1180
07	975	6	1190
06	1005	7	1210
05	1030	8	1225
04	1050	9	1250
03	1080	10	1260
02	1095	11	1285
01	1110	12	1310
		13	1350
		14	1390

159. *End points of pyrometric cones when heated at 20° C. per hour.*

The pyrometric cone has the great advantage of measuring both the effects of temperature and the length of firing on the ware in the kiln. If the firing is slow, the effect of the longer time is to cause the cones to soften at a lower temperature. The same thing happens to the ceramic ware being fired; the complex reactions of vitrification may be completed at a lower temperature if sufficient time is allowed. The ceramist is advised to put more trust in cones than in pyrometers as far as the actual condition of the fired ware is concerned. The ceramic industry continues to use cones, even though the exact temperature in the kiln is conveniently recorded by the pyrometer.

Cones are set in a plaque of fireclay. The cones should be placed so they lean about 8°, buried in the plaque no more than 2 mm. The cones are best placed close together on the plaque so they will take up less room and be visible through a small spy hole. The cone plaque should be set in the kiln some distance back from the spy hole.

Since cones melt and deform slowly, the question may arise as to when is a cone down. Technically, the cone is considered down when the tip reaches the level of the base, as shown in Figure 158. Other positions during the softening of the cone have been compared to the positions of the hand of a clock. Thus a cone at "3 o'clock" would be one which had bent over to a point where the tip could be considered to have reached 3 on the clock face.

The pyrometer came into use in the ceramic industry at about the turn of the century[1]. It is based on the discovery, in 1821, by Seebeck, who observed that if two wires of copper and iron were fused together at one end and the fused end heated, electromotive force (*e.m.f.*) was generated and a current would flow from the copper to the iron at the hot end. The flow of current varies directly with the temperature, which enables the thermocouple, as it is called, to be used for the measurement of temperature. The parts of a pyrometer are shown in Figure 160. The thermocouple *A* is connected by lead wires *B* to a galvanometer *C*, which is calibrated to indicate the temperature. The thermocouple, which is inserted into the kiln, must be protected by a porcelain sleeve.

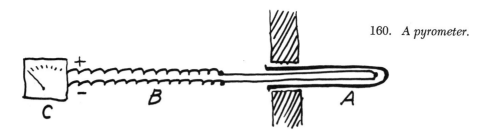

160. *A pyrometer.*

For lower temperature ceramic firing, thermocouples of chromel-alumel are used, and are serviceable up to about cone 5. The chromel wire is the positive wire. It is an alloy of approximately 90% nickel and 10% chromium. The alumel, which is the negative wire of the couple, is an alloy containing approximately 94% nickel, 2% aluminum, 3% manganese, and 1% silicon. The large amount of nickel in the alloy used in the couple aids in reducing the susceptibility of the couple to oxidation and corrosion. For high temperature firing, a thermocouple made of platinum and platinum-rhodium is used. It is made of a positive wire, containing 90% platinum and 10% rhodium, and a negative wire of pure platinum. The two wires are fused together by means of an electric arc or an oxygen-illuminating gas flame. This thermocouple has a high resistance to oxidation, and will indicate accurate temperatures up to about 1650° C. Platinum-rhodium thermocouples are expensive.

The galvanometer used to measure the current from the thermocouple must be a sensitive instrument, because the *e.m.f.* produced by the hot junction is very small. Usually a millivoltmeter of the d'Arsonval type is used. This is a standard electrical measuring instrument used for many purposes in the electrical field. Since the instrument is very delicate and must respond to a total electrical power of as low as 5 millivolts, care must be taken not to subject it to vibrations or shock, if accurate readings are expected. A more rugged indicating instrument is the

[1] For an excellent discussion of instruments available for the measurement of high temperatures, see Thomas J. Rhodes, *Industrial Instruments for Measurement and Control* (New York: Mc-Graw-Hill Inc., 1941), pp. 100–185.

161. *The kiln room at State University of New York College of Ceramics, at Alfred University.*

potentiometer, which amplifies the actual current coming from the thermocouple. Recording pyrometers use a potentiometer and a device that records the temperature in the form of a pen line on a time-temperature chart.

A pyrometer is valuable for indicating the temperatures reached at all stages of firing. The ceramist can control the advance of temperature with due regard for critical points where the firing must proceed slowly, such as the stage of firing from 570° C. to 600° C., when quartz is changing from *alpha* to the *beta* form. It is also very useful in gauging the cooling of the kiln, of which the cones tell nothing. Several thermocouples may be used with one pyrometer to obtain the temperatures in various parts of the kiln.

For extremely high temperature measurement the optical pyrometer and the total radiation pyrometer have been developed. These are based on the observation or measurement of the light or radiation coming from inside the kiln, with no part of the instrument being subjected to heat. An electrical filament is placed inside a telescope with an eye-piece. The filament is heated with a battery until its color matches the color of the inside of the kiln, as observed by pointing the instrument at the spy hole. The dial indicating temperature is calibrated to the amount of current going to the filament. Optical pyrometers are little used in pottery firing because of their expense and because the temperatures involved are usually well below the upper limits of the noble metal thermocouple. Moreover, the cloudy atmosphere of a kiln firing in reduction will give an inaccurate temperature reading on the optical pyrometer.

In order to duplicate firings, most ceramists keep a kiln log. In the log, the advance of temperature is noted, hour by hour, from pyrometer readings, and the final part of the firing is carefully logged by noting the time at which the various cones go down. Changes in burners, damper settings, and atmosphere should also be recorded.

5

Special Firing
Techniques

IN ADDITION TO the oxidizing and reducing fire, there are a number of firing methods which are of interest to studio potters. Crystaline glazes and luster glazes both require special treatment in cooling. For crystaline glazes it is necessary to hold the kiln at a certain temperature during the cooling cycle to allow the crystals to form in the glaze. The pryometer is almost a necessity if good results are expected from every firing.

Luster glazes are reduced during the cooling cycle. Any kiln that makes a dense reducing atmosphere is suitable, whether fired with gas, oil, or wood. Reduction is usually continued until the kiln just goes dark at around 580° C. For good lusters the reduction has to be quite heavy, and the damper should be kept almost closed. Electric kilns have been successfully used for luster effects. In this case, some carbonaceous material, such as oil soaked bandage rolls or moth balls, is introduced into the ware chamber during cooling.

The popularity of Raku firing has brought about a good deal of interest in kilns for this particular kind of pottery. The term "Raku" is somewhat confusing because of its several meanings. In a strict sense it refers to the pottery made by the Raku family in Japan. This line of potters originated with Chojiro, a Korean immigrant of the time of Hideoshi in the latter part of the 16th century.

Chojiro gained the patronage of Hideoshi and of the tea master Sen Riku. He was given a seal with the Chinese character "Raku" which means roughly, "happiness." From that time on he used Raku as a family name, and he and his descendants made tea wares and especially tea bowls, which were largely hand modeled rather than thrown, and which were fired at lower temperatures than the usual stoneware of the time.

Raku bowls are of two types. The red Raku is made from a reddish earthenware clay and is glazed with a lead glaze. The soft glaze over the red clay gives a warm brown to the salmon color, often with blackish markings or milky opacity where the glaze is thick. These red Raku bowls were sometimes, but not always, pulled from the kiln while red hot. The quick cooling, in any case, has little to do with the color or texture and may have originally been a technique to speed up the firing process.

The other type of Raku is the black glazed pottery. It is made from a buff stoneware clay, and the glaze is made up largely from a kind of stone found in the Kamo River near Kyoto. These black pieces are fired to a higher temperature than the red, and are always pulled from the kiln hot. The quick cooling in this case favors the rather leathery surface texture which is an important feature of the ware. Traditional Raku red and black wares are still being made by the descendants of the original Raku, and the pieces are signed with the original seal. In Japan, many pieces are also made which, although not from the hand of the Raku line of potters, carry on the original style as closely as possible, and one may buy a Raku piece in a Japanese department store for a few dollars. It may, in fact, be a very good piece.

The firing of Raku bowls has nothing to do with the tea ceremony, although the bowls certainly are made to be used for tea. The widespread misconception that Raku making is somehow a part of the tea ceremony no doubt originated from Bernard Leach's account, in *A Potter's Book*, of how he attended a party in Tokyo at which a potter fired bowls decorated by the guests in a Raku kiln in the garden. Leach indicates that the party went on "in the tea-room," but of course, he did not mean to imply that a *tea ceremony* was in progress.[1]

The term Raku is also used in Japan to denote earthenware in general, especially glazed wares used for the tea ceremony. Ogata Kenzan (1663–1743), in the diaries recently discovered and attributed to him by Leach and others, mentions Raku production as signifying all of the work he did at low fire.[2] It is not clear whether he pulled many of his pieces out of the kiln while hot, but this process, in any case, is not really the essence of Raku in Japan. In Japan, Raku could be defined as pottery made at red heat and covered with soft glaze or an enamel-like decoration, and usually consisting of tea bowls or other shapes associated with the tea ceremony.

Warren Gilbertson, who worked as an apprentice for several Japanese potters, beginning in 1938, must be credited with being the first potter to bring first-hand information about the Raku process to this country. Gilbertson exhibited his own Raku pots at the Art Institute of Chicago in 1940 and wrote an excellent article on Raku for the Bulletin of the American Ceramic Society.[3] Bernard Leach's book

---

[1] *Op. cit.*

[2] Bernard Leach, *Kenzan and His Tradition* (London: Faber and Faber, 1966).

[3] Warren Gilbertson, *Making Raku Ware*, Bulletin of the American Ceramic Society, Vol. 22 (February, 1943), p. 41.

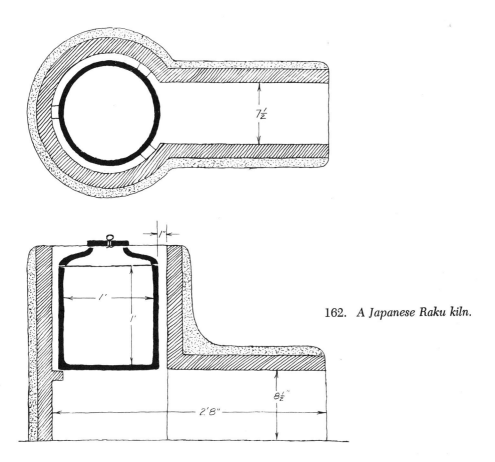

162. *A Japanese Raku kiln.*

which also appeared at this time, stimulated interest in Raku, but it was not until the middle fifties that making Raku became really popular in this country.

As one might expect, the technical side of Raku, and especially the feature of quick cooling, has become the main preoccupation of practitioners of Raku in this country. The original meaning of Raku has almost been forgotten. The more immediate response from the fire has speeded up the process of pottery making and brought a new excitement to it. Raku, which was originally an aspect of a Zen-inspired tea cult, has become a vehicle for the sudden thrust of intuition and the playing of hunches: the power of Zen still at work, perhaps. The process has yielded exciting effects and brought to earthenware a liveliness of surface which was entirely absent in the usual electric kiln products. The flaws of Raku—its softness, fragility, and permeability—can be overcome to some extent by careful body formulation and sufficiently high bisque firing. Paul Soldner, who has done a great deal of work in Raku, has developed various decorative processes based on the cooling of the ware and on carbonizing the pieces after they come out of the kiln. He has also designed and built many interesting kilns for Raku.

Figure 162 illustrates a small Japanese Raku kiln, based on dimensions given by Gilbertson. It is made up of an inner muffle with a lid that is removed to take out the fired pot. It is a very inconvenient kiln to use because of the necessity for

constant stoking with wood during the process. Much more suitable are kilns burning gas. Almost any gas kiln can be used for Raku. A section of the door is reserved for acccess to the pots inside, and is temporarily closed with insulating brick. Figure 197 shows a Raku kiln with two chambers, each with a swinging door. This is a very good kiln for class work, because if both chambers are used, two or more students can work at once. The swinging doors can be rapidly opened and closed with a minimum loss of heat. In another design, Figure 164, the kiln is built by lining a metal drum with refractory material and suspending the drum in a steel frame with a counterweight that enables the drum, burner and all to be raised off the hearth or bottom of the kiln. When the drum is raised, the fired pot is removed and a new one is placed. The drum, which has not lost much of its heat, is then lowered again. Another possibility is a small car kiln, as shown in Figure 165. In this kiln the pots are drawn out of the kiln on·a shuttle when they are finished, and another set placed and pushed back into the kiln.

164. *A Raku kiln which can be raised to remove the piece. Based on a design by Ronald Boling.*

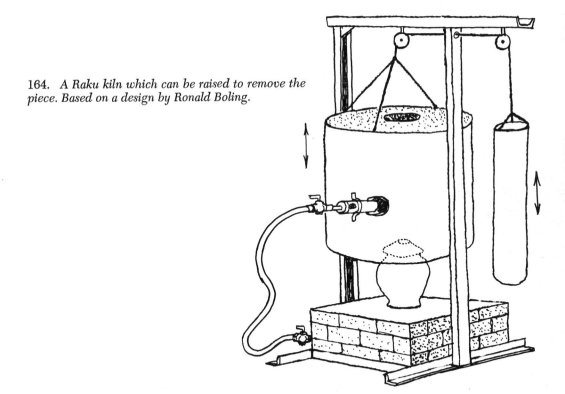

163. *Raku pot, by David Tell. The pattern of craze lines has been controlled by basting the pot with water soon after taking it from the kiln. The body of the piece has been blackened by surrounding it with straw while still red hot. Photo by David Tell.*

165. *A small shuttle kiln for Raku firing.*

166. *Shoji Hamada's salt kiln at Mashiko, Japan.*

167. *Salt kiln at Alfred, N. Y. Built by Richard Wukich in 1967.*

The electric kiln can be used for Raku, and it is very convenient because of the easy control of temperature. When the door is opened, however, the sudden change of temperature is hard on the elements. Electric kilns which have a bricked in door are better for Raku because in this case only a relatively small opening in the door is used, just big enough to get the pots in and out.

The carbon treatment of Raku pots is not done in the kiln, but may be considered part of the firing process. The red hot pot is taken from the kiln and put directly into a metal container filled with sawdust, excelsior, leaves or grass, and then the lid is closed. Strong reducing conditions develop on the surface of the piece in contact with the combustible material. The effects of this treatment are to blacken the body, sometimes erratically, and to produce luster effects in glazes containing copper. Craze marks are greatly emphasized by the carbon.

Salt glazing should be done in a good downdraft kiln that will circulate the salt vapors thoroughly through the setting. A kiln of 15 cu. ft. capacity or more is recommended. The best refractory material for a salt kiln is hard firebrick. Before the first firing this should be washed over with aluminum oxide to prevent an excessive buildup of a salt glaze on the inside of the kiln. Ports provided for introducing the salt should be positioned so the salt will fall into the combustion area ahead of the burners. An ample flue and chimney is required to carry off the unpleasant vapors, which are dangerous if allowed to accumulate indoors. The problem in salt glazing is the buildup of glaze on the kiln and the kiln furniture. Shelves, particularly, have a short life. Silicon carbide shelves should be washed with aluminum oxide to prevent slagging. Pottery should be placed in the kiln on platforms or pads made of pure kaolin, which will prevent pieces from sticking to the shelves, or the whole upper surface of the shelf may be dusted with flint before placing the pots. Hamada uses little sea shells stuffed with clay under his salt glazed pieces. After firing, the shell hydrates and disintegrates, but during the fire it keeps the bottom of the pot from sticking.

Salt kilns should be built, if possible, in some outdoor shed or other location where the fumes will not be objectionable, and the location should be such that the exhaust fumes from the chimney do not constitute a nuisance for neighbors.

6

Safety Precautions

KILN SETTING LOOKS like a safe activity, but the act of lifting heavy shelves into the kiln has caused many back injuries. It is important not to attempt to lean into the kiln with a heavy shelf in your hands. Better to crawl into the kiln, if it is large enough, and have someone hand in the shelf.

Although kilns operate at a high temperature, they need not be fire hazards. In fact, surprisingly few fires originate from ceramic kilns. The heat, while intense, is confined in a secure and insulated zone, and nothing short of the collapse of the entire kiln, an unlikely circumstance, would subject the room to the direct effects of the heat of the kiln. Obviously, kilns need to be built in ways that totally preclude the possibility of their collapse during firing.

Certain safety precautions must be taken. Especially important is the chimney and the manner in which the chimney passes through the roof, or other parts of a building. Most of the fires which have started from kiln firing have been caused by faulty construction of the flashing around the chimney. The masonry construction of the chimney should be separated from the wood rafters, roof or ceiling by at least 8 inches, and preferably more, and some ventilation around the chimney is necessary to keep it cool during firing.

When lighting gas burners, it is important to place the fire or torch against the opening of the burner before turning on the gas. If burners go out, plenty of time must be allowed before trying to relight the kiln, to be sure there is no gas in the chamber.

It is advisable to have a shutoff valve on the gas line at some distance from the kiln. Then, in case of fire, gas to all the burners may be cut off at once. Another sensible precaution is to have a sizable fire extinguisher handy in the kiln room.

Too many kilns are crammed into spaces which are inadequate. It is important to have enough room around the kiln to work, and there should be plenty of space especially around the burners. But kilns are usually built in already existing spaces that were not planned for them, where this prescription cannot be followed. Certainly low ceilings and walls too close to the kiln constitute a fire hazard.

Ventilation is another important consideration. Fuel burning kilns always give off a certain amount of gas, even when they are fired in oxidation. Even electric kilns emit gases originating from the changes in the ware being fired. In reduction firing, considerable amounts of carbon monoxide and carbon dioxide are sure to escape into the room. Carbon monoxide, which is odorless, is a lethal gas, and breathing even small amounts of it is considered unhealthy. A window fan or roof vent with a fan will draw off the fumes and bring in fresh air. With reduction firing there is always a certain amount of smoke that may blacken walls and ceilings, and a fan helps to prevent this as well as evacuating undesirable gas.

There are a few personal safety precautions to take when working around kilns. Loose clothing, scarves, and the like should be avoided because of the danger of their catching on fire from burner ports or spy holes. Care must be taken peering into spy holes to avoid the danger of flame injuring the eyes or face. Dark glasses should be worn to avoid eye injury from radiation from the inside of a kiln heated to 1200° C. or more. In any case, dark glasses make it easier to see the cones in high firing. Care must also be taken that plastic spectacle lenses or contact lenses are not damaged by exposure to the radiant heat of the spy holes or burner ports.

The most usual accident in the kiln room is a burn suffered from picking up a piece which is still too hot. In view of the eagerness with which potters get acquainted with their new pots, this is a perennial problem. Strictly speaking the kiln should not be opened until it has cooled down to about 250° C. at which time the ware will quickly cool and be easy to handle with a pair of asbestos mittens.

7

The Potter
and His Kiln

*"Fire is the ultra-living element. It is intimate and it is univer-
sal. It lives in our heart. It lives in the sky. It rises from the depths of the substance and
offers itself with the warmth of love. Or it can go back down into the substance and hide
there, latent and pent-up, like hate and vengeance. Among all phenomenon, it is really
the only one to which there can be so definitely attributed the opposing values of good
and evil. It shines in Paradise. It burns in Hell."*

Gaston Bachelard[1]

For potters, the firing process has always been a matter of intense concern, perhaps because of the uncertainties attending it. In the past, many superstitions grew
up about it, and in China and Japan, the firing was frequently turned over to
specialists. In some Japanese pottery villages, women were not allowed to go near
the firing kiln. In every culture, we may be sure, divine power has been invoked
for the success of the firing, and kiln gods, prayer sticks, and offerings have been
common. Piccolpasso describes the lighting of the kiln as follows, ". . . invoking the
name of God, take a handful of straw, and with the sign of the cross light the
fire. . . ."[2]

Today, while we may curse the results of a firing, we seldom pray for its success.
But firing retains its mystery and its power. Placing one's pieces in the kiln is a kind
of surrender, a giving up to the metamorphic forces of the fire. In the early stages
of the fire, the pot suffers a kind of death; its substance undergoes at first a
deterioration and weakening of structure. With his best efforts in this limbo, the

---

[1] Gaston Bachelard, *The Psychoanalysis of Fire* (Boston: Beacon Press, 1964), p. 7. Trans. Alan
C. M. Ross.

[2] Piccolpasso, *op. cit.*

potter feels on the one hand a sense of estrangement from his work, and on the other a keener identification with it. As the fire advances, he may sense a participation in the action of the intense heat. The hours during which the kiln is firing may be spent in routine tasks or in a kind of reassessment of values and directions. The firing gives a natural periodicity to pottery making, a time when one cycle is ending and another not yet begun. All ceramists feel a sense of excitement when the kiln is opened, but most also experience a feeling of letdown and depression after the pieces have all been removed from the kiln and inspected. It is the same feeling which comes over children on Christmas night, when there is nothing more to look forward to. Expectation has been replaced by certainty and possession.

Undoubtedly the most important skills in pottery making have to do with shaping, glazing, and formulation of the materials, but the importance of the firing process and its relation to creative work should not be underemphasized. Many potters experience a great improvement in the quality of their work and in the satisfaction in it when they take over the complete job of firing, rather than having it done for them by teachers or by collaborating groups. Firing is critical, and when it is successful the fruits of all the other processes are reaped. But by the same token, if it fails all else is canceled and counts for nothing. It is the make-or-break phase of the whole process.

Firing can be reduced to a more or less fixed routine, so that each firing is exactly the same as the one before. In this case, typical in industry, there would seem to be little in it that is creative. It is then merely the repetition of a fixed method or firing cycle which was originally found to give good results. If firing is routinized, the only surprises on opening the kiln will be the failures. But for the individual potter making relatively small quantities of ware, firing can seldom be reduced to a repeatable system. Many variables work against the complete regularization of firing. Among these are the differences in setting, in the shelf arrangement, in the variety of the pieces in size and shape, and even in the weather, which may affect the draft. Because there is much at stake, potters the world over have striven for uniformity and predictability in firing, but they have, at least until modern times, achieved it in only a limited way. A story is told by Bernard Palissy, the famous French potter of the 16th Century, of how he tore up the floors of his house for fuel to finish a firing. Surely something had gone wrong to require this unexpected need for more fuel.

The many possible variables, and the likelihood of unfortunate accidents to the ware have brought considerable anxiety to the firing process. Even where anxiety is allayed by confidence or indifference, the suspense remains. The suspense of awaiting the final results of one's labors with the opening of the kiln is the central experience of the ceramist. A wonderful scene in the Japanese film *Ugetsu* powerfully conveys this feeling. In the film, the pottery village is overrun by an invading army just when the potters are firing and are bringing their huge kiln to its climax of temperature. The potters flee, fearing that all is ruined since they were unable

168. *Old Tamba jar. Japanese, Muromachi period (1336–1573). This piece was fired in a primitive bank kiln, as shown in Figure 19, and owes its beautiful green glaze entirely to the deposit of ash during the firing process.*

169. *Old Tamba jar. Japanese, Muromachi period (1336–1573). Collection, National Museum of Art, Kyoto, Japan. Natural ash deposit glaze. The clay tabs toward the bottom were added by the kiln setter to make the piece fit snuggly into the one below.*

170. *Old Tamba jar. Japanese, Muromachi period (1336–1573). Collection, Dr. Seiki, Kyoto, Japan. Natural ash deposit glaze. The scars on the piece resulted from being stuck to another pot during firing. The roughness on the shoulder was caused by fragments dropping onto the piece from the ceiling of the kiln.*

171. *Tokoname jar. Japanese, Kamakura Period (1192–1573). Collection, Tokoname Ceramic Center. A natural ash deposit glaze has run down the sides of the piece.*

172. *Old Bizen jar. Japanese, Muromachi Period (1336–1573). Collection, National Museum of Art, Kyoto, Japan. The beautiful markings result from the print of straw in which the piece was set during firing.*

173. *Ceramic, "Untitled," by Karen Karnes. From the exhibit "The Object Transformed," Museum of Modern Art, 1967. A kiln accident has resulted in a work of art of compelling power. Photo, Museum of Modern Art.*

to give the kiln its last "soaking" of heat to bring out the beauty of the glazes. The soldiers poke at the hot kiln but do not really molest it. The next day, after the soldiers have moved on, the potters open the kiln in an agony of suspense. A miracle! The ware has not been harmed by the interrupted firing and is, in fact, much more beautiful than they had hoped.

All potters try to visualize their finished work as they peer through the spy holes into the incandescent interior of the kiln. The fusing heat, bathing everything in a uniform light, is like some generic force, the more to be respected because its ways are not perfectly understood. One might think that the potter's dream of his finished work would excel in beauty and interest the pieces which he actually takes from the kiln the next day. But often the kiln confers graces on the pot which exceed even the potter's dreams. The greatest pots are those one meets coming from the kiln as strange objects; they may seem, in texture and color, quite beyond one's power to visualize or predict.

To be a ceramist is to not only understand but to feel this transformation of the fire, and to be able to live with it, to work with it, and to collaborate with it. The job of firing the kiln is actually quite complex. It requires knowledge and judgement, and only experience will enable the kiln watcher to cope with the unexpected and to make those small adjustments that may mean the difference between failure and success, or between success and triumph. To work with the fire creatively requires an understanding of its action. Every phase of pottery making is enriched by such an understanding. In fact, the potter is working with the fire even as he designs pieces to withstand its heat and as he gauges the thickness and character of slips and glazes, with their tendency to run, to flow, to reveal, to conceal. Such insights into the ways of the fire make pottery the art that it is.

PART 4

Kiln Designs

Kiln Designs

In MOST CASES kiln designs must be adapted to a particular location and to specific needs, but it is hoped that the designs given here will help as a general guide to various possibilities. The designs are all rather easy to build. No attempt is made to give an estimate of cost, since local prices may vary considerably. To estimate the number of bricks required for a given design, the volume of the floor, walls, crown, and chimney is calculated in cubic inches. This figure, the total volume of brickwork, is then divided by 100, the approximate number of cubic inches in one 9-inch straight brick. About 10% should be added for loss in cutting, etc.

Most of the designs can be changed in size without fear of impairing the effectiveness of the kiln, provided that the general proportions are held to, and provided sufficient burner capacity is installed. Except for the wood burning kilns, all the designs are intended for gas, either natural gas or LPG, but any of the larger kilns could be fired with oil.

Before building a kiln one first should look at and study other existing kilns, if possible. Much can be learned from first hand inspection, and copying an existing kiln which fires well gives some assurance of success. Since the investment required to build a kiln is considerable, many prospective kiln builders are deterred by fear of failure. While a certain amount of anxiety is justified, it is the author's experience that most kilns perform satisfactorily provided they are designed with consideration for a few basic, common sense principles, and provided there is sufficient fuel burning capacity.

There are two reasons for building a kiln rather than buying one. One is the savings in money. A do-it-yourself kiln will cost only a fraction of what one must

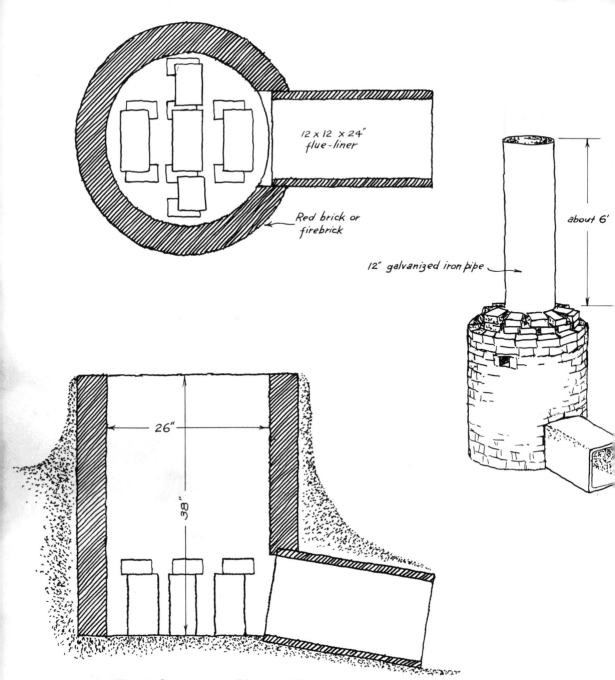

12 x 12 x 24"
flue-liner

Red brick or
firebrick

about 6'

12" galvanized iron pipe

26"

38"

174. *Rudimentary wood burning kiln.*

pay to buy, ship, and install a portable kiln. The other reason is the great amount of satisfaction to be derived from building a successful kiln.

Figure 174 is a simple updraft kiln suitable for a camp or class project. It is very similar to early Mediterranean kilns such as are still in use in Crete. The drum shape of the kiln can be made of red brick, firebrick, or sandstone smeared with clay inside. The bricks can be layed in a circle for each course and the wedge-shaped spaces between bricks filled with clay. The kiln can be built right on the ground, with some sand placed in the bottom before firing. The fire mouth is made from a flue liner set at an upward slope. The bottom part of the kiln may be partially banked up with earth for additional insulation.

The pots are set up on a shelf arrangement to allow the fire to sweep in at the bottom of the cylinder. Plenty of space must be allowed for the upward circulation of the fire. The top of the kiln is closed over by corbeling in several courses of bricks, with a hole left at the top. A length of galvanized pipe placed over the hole forms a chimney to increase the draft.

A kiln of this sort will reach earthenware temperature with ease, although the bottom is sure to fire hotter than the top. It is certainly not good for exacting work with glazes, but a simple fritted glaze for cone 04, used, perhaps over slips, should work reasonably well. The kiln could easily be built in one day, and if scrap materials are used, the cost will be next to nothing.

Figure 175 is a more elaborate outdoor kiln, also for wood firing. It is based on the principle of the Korean kiln; that is, a sloping trench with fire introduced at the bottom and along the sides. A hillside with an incline of about 20 to 25 degrees is required. The length is somewhat optional, but a tunnel of about 16 feet in length will give an excellent draft. Attached to the lower part of the kiln is the main

175. *Wood burning trench kiln.*

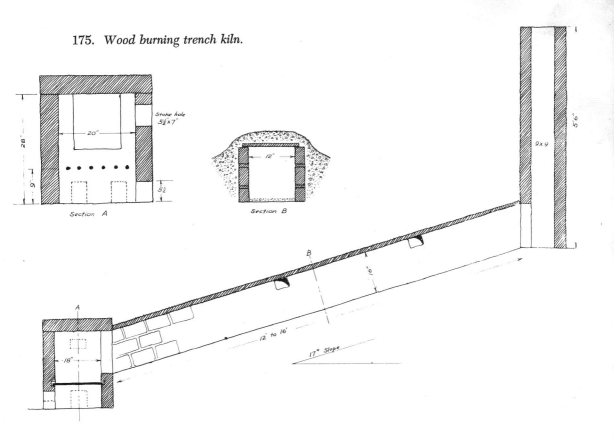

177. *Starting the walls of the trench and the firebox. The bricks are placed directly on the ground.*

176. *Digging the trench in the hillside. Photo by Ed Custer.*

178. *Construction of the firebox and ware chamber. The notches will hold the metal grate rods.*

firebox. It is built in the form of a simple rectangle, with a suspended roof of insulating brick, as shown. It may be built with an arched roof. The grate bars are steel rods. The ware chamber is a trench lined on the sides with brick and roofed over with kiln shelves. An alternate construction is a corbeled structure closed over at the top with one 9-inch firebrick. A short chimney is built at the end of the chamber. One or two additional stokeholes along the tunnel are piled with wood during the firing to increase the temperature in the upper part of the kiln. A group of students working with me at Alfred built a kiln of this type and fired it successfully to cone 9, in the lower third of the kiln, with lower temperatures above. We used dry bass wood and hemlock for fuel, completing the firing in about 12 hours. The pots near the firemouth were heavily encrusted with fly-ash glaze and closely resembled Japanese Bizen wares in color and texture. More protected pieces developed successful celadon glazes. Rather heavy reducing conditions prevailed in the lower half of the kiln.

179. *Finishing the firebox. Photo by Ed Custer.*

181. *The top of the kiln is covered over with dirt. Photo by Ed Custer.*

The kiln takes quite a few bricks to build, and can hardly be justified as a design unless scrap bricks are available. It is essentially a temporary kiln, fun to build and very exciting to fire.

To load the kiln, sand is placed on the floor, and the pots are set in rows, smaller pieces stacked one on another. The covering slabs are then put in place, and earth

180. *Setting the kiln. Photo by Ed Custer.*

182. *Opening the kiln. The supplementary stoke holes can be seen at the right of the chamber. Photo by Ed Custer.*

is heaped up over the whole structure. About two inches of dirt over the slabs provides ample insulation. Additional draft can be induced by adding a section of galvanized iron pipe to the chimney. For lower temperature work this is not necessary, because the upward slope of the chamber makes for a good draft.

Figure 183 is a small updraft kiln. It is vented directly into the room or, if it is being fired in a confined space without adequate ventilation, a hood is provided to carry off the waste gases. The kiln is built of K-26 insulating brick, mortared together with thin fireclay cement. The skews and arch brick are shaped by hand. The kiln is held together with a light angle iron frame, and the bottom rests on a piece of asbestos cement board. A metal plate could be used for the bottom. Four gas burners are arranged at the sides. They should be securely fastened to the frame of the kiln. The whole front of the kiln is considered a door and is bricked in each time. The first kiln shelf is held up off the floor on 2½-inch props. The

183. *Gas-fired updraft kiln.*

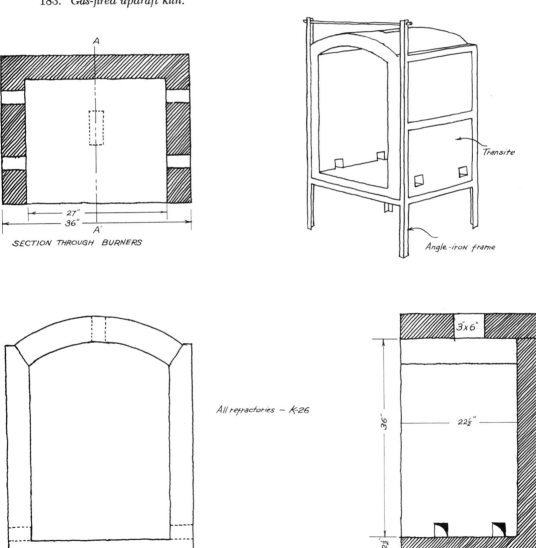

SECTION THROUGH BURNERS

27"
36"

Transite

Angle-iron frame

All refractories — K-26

FRONT   Transite

3"x 6"

36"   22½"

2½"

SECTION A-A'

burners are baffled to send most of their flame up along the walls, but some of the flame is directed to the bottom of the shelf. This kiln is inexpensive and very easy to build. It will fire rapidly if desired. Some unevenness of temperature is to be expected between top and bottom, and reduction may be spotty, especially towards the center of the setting. A kiln of this type must be set rather openly and the interior space not choked off too much by the kiln shelves. In spite of the compact over-all size of the kiln, it has a very good capacity. It is extremely easy to load

184. *Gas-fired downdraft kiln.*

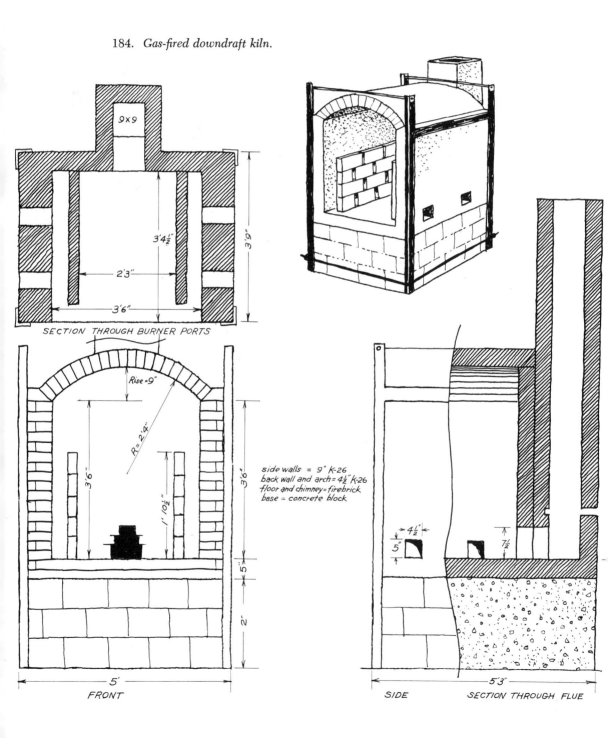

SECTION THROUGH BURNER PORTS

9×9

3'4½"

2'3"

3'6"

3'9"

Rise = 9"

R = 2'4"

3'6"

3'6"

1'10½"

5"

2'

side walls = 9" K-26
back wall and arch = 4½" K-26
floor and chimney = firebrick
base = concrete block

4½"

5"

7½"

5'

FRONT

SIDE   SECTION THROUGH FLUE

5'3"

and to fire. The draft may be increased by building a short chimney of five or six courses of brick on top of the kiln.

The virtues of this updraft design are its ease of building and the large amount of usable space per cubic inch of kiln structure. Many commercially produced portable kilns are of essentially the same design. The disadvantages are uneven heating and rather uncertain reduction, but both of these drawbacks can be more or less overcome by intelligent setting of shelves and ware.

Shown in Figure 184 is a downdraft kiln built mostly from insulating brick. It is a fairly good sized kiln with walls 9 inches thick. The kiln is built on a platform of concrete block over which are laid two thicknesses of firebrick. The walls are made of K-26 brick laid in thin mortar. The skewbacks and shaped brick for the arch can be easily cut by hand. A light steel frame is provided to take the thrust of the arch. The front of the kiln is left open, and is bricked in for each firing. The bag wall, made of hard firebrick, is formed from brick set on edge. Ample chinks are left between the bricks of the bag wall, which can be partially filled with fragments of insulating brick after experimenting with the flame patterns of the kiln. Four burners, of 150,000 B.t.u. per hour rating, should be sufficient.

A kiln of this type should produce perfect results in reduction firing, and can be made to fire evenly by proper adjustments of the height and permeability of the bag walls. The capacity is about eighteen cubic feet.

Figure 185 shows a larger kiln, designed for permanent installation and long life. The interior of the kiln is made entirely of hard firebrick, backed up by a layer of insulation and an outer case of red brick. The finished structure is handsome, and may be cleaned of soot from time to time to give a good appearance in schools or studio. The collecting flue is set in a trough extending from the front to the back of the kiln. The arch is 9 inches thick, made from wedge brick. A frame of angle irons and tie rods furnishes the exterior bracing.

The base is made of concrete block or red brick, with a channel provided for the flue. Next, a layer of firebrick is placed for the floor of the kiln. The walls are started, and the hard brick course inside and the red brick outside are carried along at the same time. The side walls are brought up to the level of the skewbacks, while the back and the front walls are still uncompleted. The skewback is set, together with its angle iron backing. Next, the arch support is put in place and the arch is made. Then the back wall is completed. The arch form for the door is put in place and the front wall is finished. With the main part of the kiln completed, the chimney is constructed next. The external bracing of the kiln is set in place and tightened. The final step is the construction of the bag walls and the placing of the floor tiles and damper.

The insulating layer between the two brick walls of the kiln may be made by slicing K-20 bricks in two lengthwise, making a layer of $1\frac{1}{4}$ inches. Or, a paste of vermiculite and clay can be made to fill the space. An occasional tie between the two walls, formed by extending a firebrick over into the red brick layer, helps give stability to the walls. Fireclay mortar is used for the inside of the kiln, and regular cement mortar is used to lay the red brick outer layer. The courses of firebrick and red brick should be kept level at all times. The chimney is made of an inner liner of hard firebrick and an outside layer of red brick without any insulation between them. After the kiln is finished, the red brick exterior can be brushed with a weak solution of muriadic acid to remove smears of mortar and to freshen up the color of the brick work.

185. *Large gas-fired downdraft kiln.*

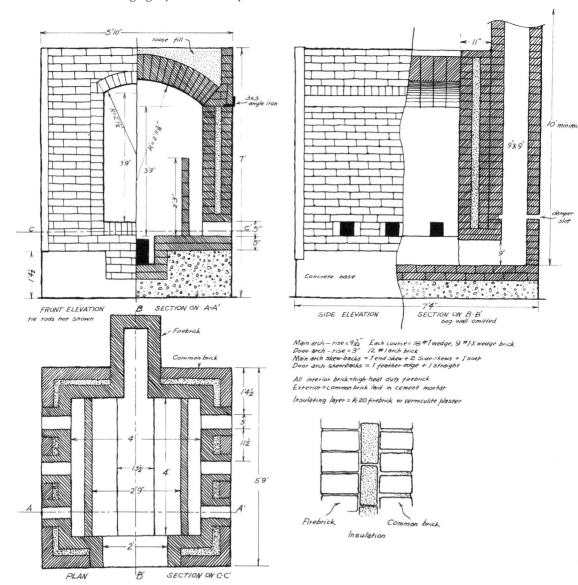

Main arch – rise = $9\frac{3}{32}''$ Each course = 18 #1 wedge, 9 #1-X wedge brick
Door arch – rise = 3"   12 #1 arch brick
Main arch skew-backs = 1 end skew + 2 side skews + 1 soap
Door arch skew-backs = 1 feather edge + 1 straight

All interior brick = high-heat duty firebrick
Exterior = common brick laid in cement mortar

Insulating layer = K-20 firebrick or vermiculite plaster

Figure 186 shows a small catenary arch kiln which uses a minimum of insulating bricks and is, therefore, quite inexpensive to build. As shown in the photographs, the arch is constructed on a base of concrete blocks topped with two layers of hard brick. The back wall is built under the arch. The front wall is bricked in for each firing, except for some bricks at the side which may be left in place more or less permanently. A 4½-inch layer of insulating bricks is used over the upper part of the arch, and a waterproof coating is applied to the exterior.

This kiln has a typical catenary arch design, and could be enlarged without

186. *Small catenary arch gas-fired downdraft kiln.*

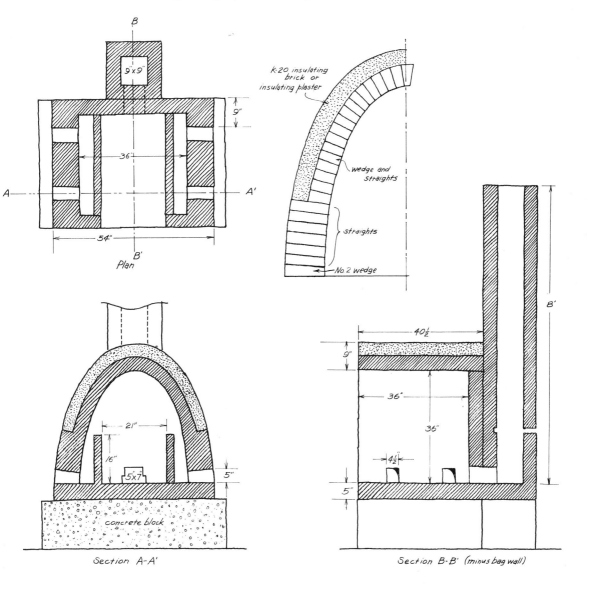

187. *Construction detail, showing the arch support form.*

188. *Arch detail.*

189. *Pulling out the arch form.*

189-A. *Building the back wall.*

190. *Construction of the damper slot.*

191. *View of the kiln and chimney from above.*

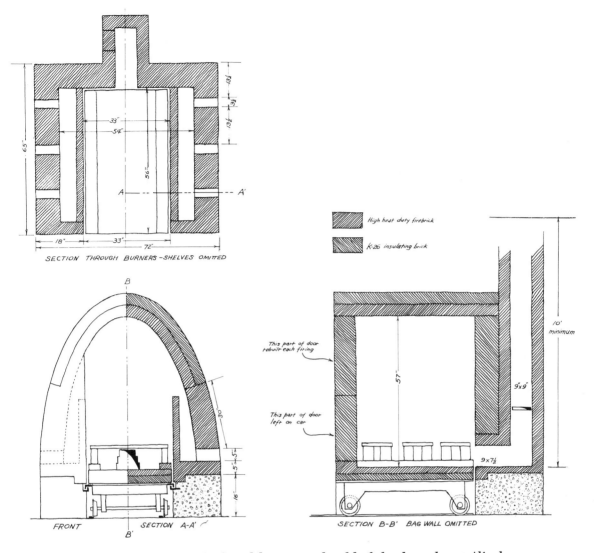

High heat duty firebrick

K-26 insulating brick

SECTION THROUGH BURNERS –SHELVES OMITTED

FRONT   SECTION A-A'

This part of door rebuilt each firing

This part of door left on car

SECTION B-B' BAG WALL OMITTED

193. *Catenary arch gas-fired car kiln. Designed and built by the author at Alfred in 1961.*

changing the general arrangement of parts, except of course for the addition of more burners. The design is very direct and simple, with no unnecessary concessions to appearance or tradition, and the fact that exterior bracing is not required makes for lower cost, as well as stability and a long life.

Figure 193 shows a car kiln incorporating a catenary arch. This design is identical to a kiln that I built in my studio in 1961, in which I have since fired both sculptures and pottery. It is fitted with 6 "Alfred" burners, similar to that shown in Figure 78, which operate on 7 oz. of pressure.

The construction of this kiln is very similar to that of the smaller catenary kiln described above. The concrete base in this case is built in a "U" shape to admit the car. Steel channels are set into the structure to form a sand seal with a skirt on the car, as shown in the drawing.

192. *The finished kiln. A waterproof blanket of cement has been applied to the exterior. Built by Ellis and Janina Jacobs, Cupertino, Calif., from a design by the author. Photos 187–192 by Janina Jacobs.*

The kiln can be finished first, making sure that the opening where the car enters is a true rectangle. The under part of the car, with its wheels and platform for the brick floor can then be designed. For the car I used wheels salvaged from an old saw mill carriage. The car has a layer of asbestos cement board over the metal framework and two layers of insulating firebrick on top of that. The wheels of the car ride directly on the concrete floor. Two guides of strap iron are fastened to the floor to guide the car into place. Since there is no track, the car can be wheeled about in the studio, which is very convenient if large sculptures are to be built in place on it.

Figure 194 shows a kiln built of K-26 insulating brick laid without mortar. The kiln has a roof of suspended insulating brick. Four burners are provided, and the

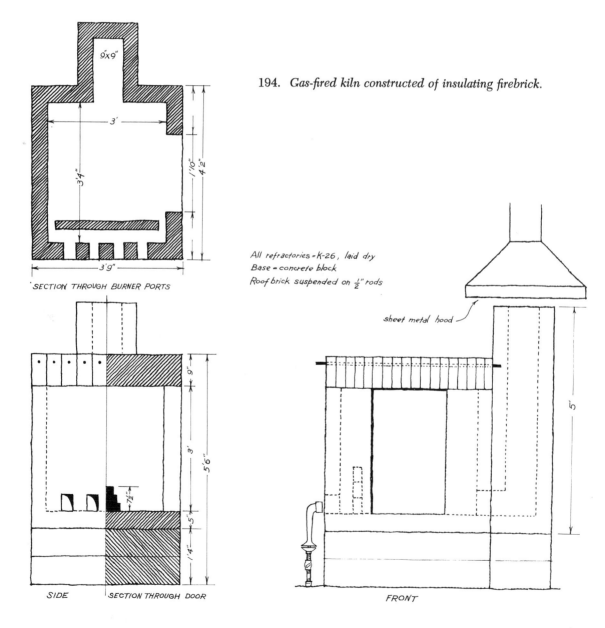

194. *Gas-fired kiln constructed of insulating firebrick.*

All refractories = K-26, laid dry
Base = concrete block
Roof brick suspended on ½" rods

circulation is essentially crossdraft. A small baffle is set ahead of the burners to deflect the flames upward. Some experimentation with the setting and with the baffling of the flame will be necessary to arrive at a good heat distribution. A hood is used to collect the exhaust gases from the short chimney.

One of the virtues of this style kiln is the ease of building. The whole kiln can be erected and ready to use in a day's time. Another advantage is that changes can be readily made—a few courses, for instance, can be added to the top to secure more interior capacity if desired. In use, the bricks may move somewhat. The usual tendency is for the structure to grow outwards, in which case the bricks are pushed back into position.

A kiln of this sort can easily be revised, in case it does not work satisfactorily.

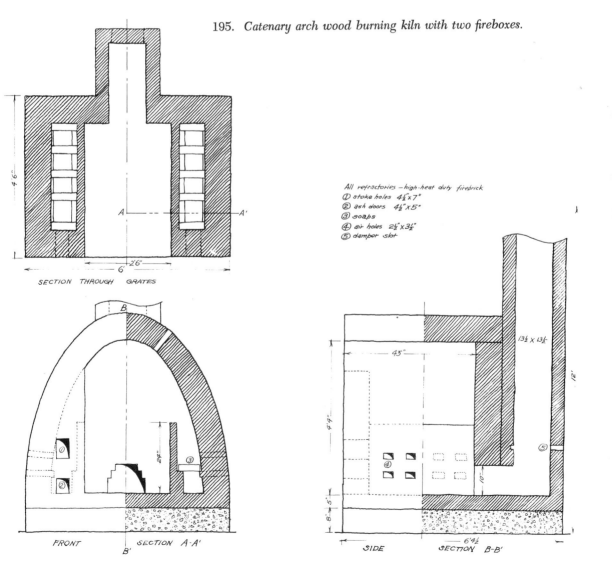

195. *Catenary arch wood burning kiln with two fireboxes.*

For example, more burners can be added, or the position of the flue and chimney changed with only minor inconvenience. This is not a cheap kiln to build, however, because of the large number of insulating firebricks required.

Shown in Figure 195 is a catenary kiln, designed to burn wood in two fireplaces at the sides. It is similar in construction to the car kiln described above. Fireboxes at either side make for a very even distribution of heat. A relatively tall chimney is indicated to assure a good draft; without it, there is not much prospect of reaching

196. *Catenary arch wood burning kiln with one firebox.*

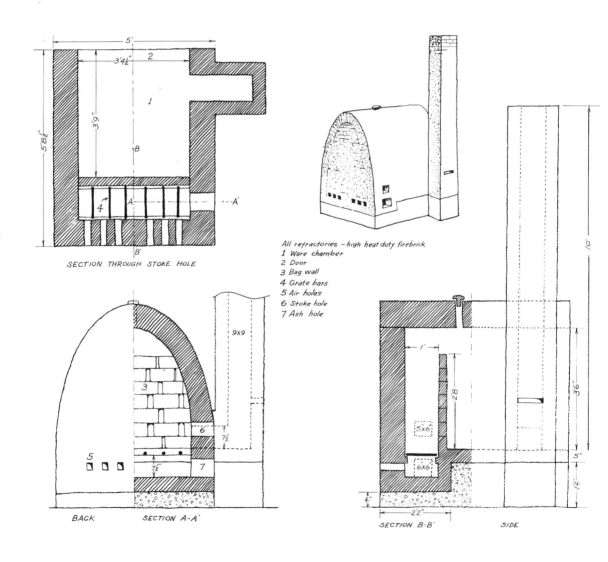

SECTION THROUGH STOKE HOLE

All refractories – high heat duty firebrick
1 Ware chamber
2 Door
3 Bag wall
4 Grate bars
5 Air holes
6 Stoke hole
7 Ash hole

BACK   SECTION A-A'

SECTION B-B'   SIDE

higher temperatures. It is not advisable to add any more horizontal flue than is shown in the drawing. The shape of the kiln is well adapted to the fireboxes and to the circulation plan.

If this design has a flaw, it is the nuisance of tending two separate fireboxes during firing.

Figure 196 shows a smaller wood-fired kiln, also of catenary arch design, having one firebox. The circulation is essentially crossdraft, and some cool spots may be

197. *Gas-fired Raku kiln with two chambers. Designed and built by David Tell.*

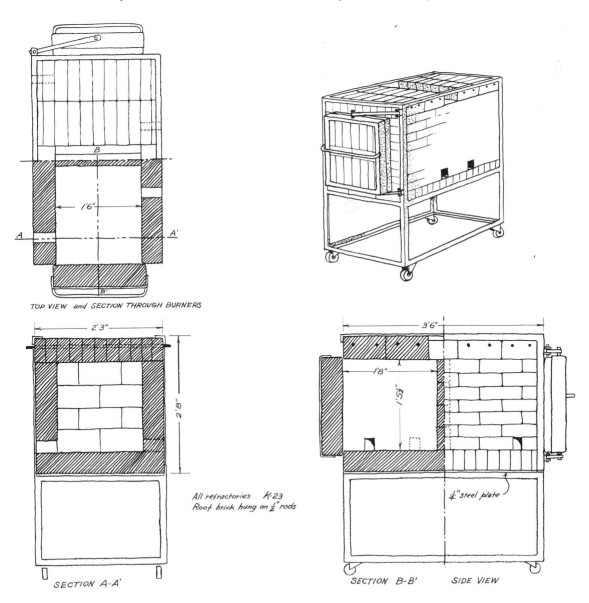

TOP VIEW *and* SECTION THROUGH BURNERS

All refractories K-23
Roof brick hung on ½" rods

SECTION A-A'

SECTION B-B'   SIDE VIEW

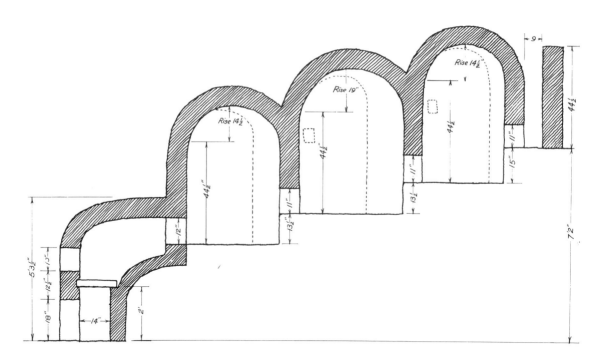

198.   *Three-chambered wood burning kiln built for the Kyoto City College of Fine Arts, Kyoto, Japan. Although rather small in size, this design has all the typical features of the Japanese* noburigama, *or chambered climbing kiln. It was built in 1963.*

199.   *View during construction.*

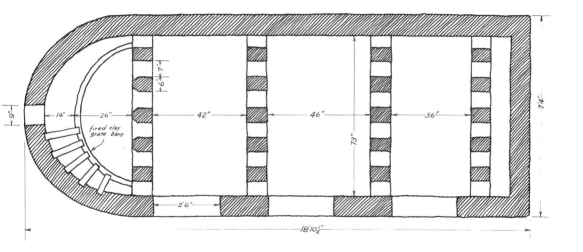

200. *Work has started on the firemouth. The holes leading into the first chamber are clearly evident. The wood brace furnishes a buttress for the first chamber until the firemouth is complete.*

201. *Construction of the firemouth. The level of the grate bars has been reached.*

202. *Back wall of the third chamber, with flues. The construction of the arch from cylindrical brick can be seen.*

203. *Arch support. Photos 199–203 by Nobusuke Eto.*

expected near the flue side of the kiln. This is perhaps the smallest size kiln which should be built for wood firing.

Figure 197 shows a kiln designed specifically for Raku firing. It has a substantial angle iron frame and two swinging doors opening into the two chambers, which can be fired separately or simultaneously. This kiln was designed by David Tell.

Figure 198 is a dimensioned drawing of a small chamber kiln built in Kyoto, Japan. It is built right on the ground with no foundation, and no insulation is used. The pictures of construction give some indication of the rather casual brick work common in Japan.

> *"Even if I used a thousand reams of paper to write down all the accidents that have happened to me in learning this art, you must be assured that, however good a brain you may have, you will still make a thousand mistakes, which cannot be learned from writings, and even if you had them in writing you wouldn't believe them until practice has given you a thousand afflictions."**
>
> —Bernard Palissy

* *Op. cit.*

Bibliography

Bachelard, Gaston. *The Psychoanalysis of Fire.* Tr. by Alan C. M. Ross. Boston: The Beacon Press, 1964.

Chang, Isabelle. *Chinese Cooking Made Easy.* New York: Liveright, 1959.

Corder, Philip. "The Structure of Romano-British Pottery Kilns," *Archeological Journal.* MXIV, 1957.

Diderot, Denis. *A Diderot Pictorial Encyclopedia of Trades and Industry.* New York: Dover Publications, Inc., 1959 [1793].

Gilbertson, Warren. "Making Raku Ware," *Bulletin of the American Ceramic Society.* XXII, February, 1943.

Hampe, Roland, and Winter, Adam. *Bei Töpfern und Topferinnen in Kreta, Messennien und Zypern.* Mainz: Verlag des Romisch-Germanischen Zentralmuseums Mainz, 1962, In Kommission Bei Rudolf Habelt Verlag, Bonn.

Harbison-Walker Refractories Company. *Modern Refractory Practice.* 4th ed. Pittsburgh, Penna.: 1961.

Kiln Drawings and Material Lists. Alfred, N. Y.: State University of New York, College of Ceramics, 1965.

Leach, B. H. *A Potter's Book.* New York: Transatlantic Arts, 1948.

————.*Kenyan and His Tradition.* London: Faber and Faber, 1966.

Nelson, G. C. *Ceramics: A Potter's Handbook.* New York: Holt, Rinehart and Winston, 1966.

Noble, Joseph V. *The Techniques of Painted Attic Pottery.* New York: Watson-Guptill, 1965.

Norton, F. H. *Ceramics for the Artist Potter.* Cambridge, Mass.: Addison-Wesley, 1956.

————. *Elements of Ceramics.* Cambridge, Mass.: Addison-Wesley, 1952.

————. *Refractories.* New York: McGraw-Hill, 1949.

Palissy, Bernard. "The Art of the Earth," *The Admirable Discourses of Bernard Palissy.* Urbana, Illinois: The University of Illinois Press, 1957.

Piccolpasso, Cipriano. *The Three Books of the Potter's Art.* London: Victoria and Albert Museum, 1934.

Rhodes, Daniel. *Clay and Glazes for the Potter*. Philadelphia: Chilton Book Company, 1957.

——. *Stoneware and Porcelain*. Philadelphia: Chilton Book Company, 1959.

Rhodes, T. J. *Industrial Instruments for Measurement and Control*. New York: McGraw-Hill, 1941.

Shepard, A. O. *Ceramics for the Archeologist*. Washington: Carnegie Institution of Washington, 1956.

Searle, A. B. *Kilns and Kiln Building*. London: The Clayworker Press, 1915.

Soldner, Paul. *Kiln Construction*. New York: American Craftsmen's Council, 1965.

Thring, M. W. *The Science of Flames and Furnaces*, 2d. ed. London: Chapman and Hall, 1962.

Wulff, Hans E. *The Traditional Crafts of Persia*. Cambridge, Mass.: M.I.T. Press, 1966.

Index

Daniel Rhodes

DANIEL RHODES, currently Professor of Ceramic Art at Alfred University, is a leading potter, sculptor and writer. He is the author of numerous articles on ceramics, and his two books, both published by Chilton, *Clay and Glazes for the Potter* and *Stoneware and Porcelain,* have become standard reference sources for potters throughout the world.

The early years of Mr. Rhodes' career in art were devoted to painting. He attended the Art Institute of Chicago and the University of Chicago, and later the Art Students League in New York. While working at the Colorado Springs Fine Arts Center, however, he became interested in ceramics. In 1941, Mr. Rhodes came East to spend a year studying at the New York State College of Ceramics at Alfred University. He became a member of the faculty of that school in 1947. Following this, his reputation as one of the country's leading ceramists spread. He was given a Fulbright Research Grant to study the arts of Japan in 1962, the position of Editorial Consultant on ceramics for the national craft magazine *Craft Horizons,* and most recently, a place in the annual sculpture exhibit of the Whitney Museum of American Art. A one-man show of his works was held at the Museum of Contemporary Crafts in New York in 1967.

Mr. Rhodes and his wife Lillyan, also a sculptor, live and work near Alfred, New York, in wooded acreage overlooking the foothills of the Allegheny Mountains.